·THE·
INTERNATIONAL
SAMPLER
COOKBOOK

Favorite Recipes Press

Great American Opportunities, Inc./Favorite Recipes Press

Editorial Staff

Editorial Manager: Mary Jane Blount
Editors: Georgia Brazil, Mary Cummings,
Jane Hinshaw, Linda Jones,
Mary Wilson
Typography: Pam Newsome

Photography

Cover: Argo/Kingsford's Corn Starch;
The J. M. Smucker Company;
The McIlhenny Company;
Hershey Foods Corporation; and
The Dow Chemical Company,
makers of SARAN WRAP™
brand plastic film

Library of Congress Catalog Number: 88-21740

ISBN: 0-87197-236-0

Manufactured in the United States of America

First Printing: 1988, 25,000 copies
Second Printing: 1988, 25,000 copies
Third Printing: 1989, 25,000 copies
Fourth Printing: 1989, 25,000 copies
Fifth Printing: 1990, 35,000 copies
Sixth Printing: 1996, 50,000 copies

TABLE OF CONTENTS

Index Of Contributors

Terra Avril
Du Quoin HS, Du Quoin, IL
Jenifer Banks
Topeka HS, Topeka, KS
Sharon Beaver
Eastbrook HS, Marion, IN
Lynn Brady
Dracut HS, Dracut, MA
Phyllis Buechfiel
Ponca City HS, Ponca City, OK
Laotha Carswell
Evans HS, Evans, GA
Gail Heffner Charles
Walnut Ridge HS, Columbus, OH
Joan M. Daniels
Sumner Acad of Arts & Sci, Kansas City, KS
Erika Daughterty
West Craven HS, Vanceboro, N.C.
Graciela R. Delgado
El Paso, TX
Jubinne S. Erickson
West Carrollton Jr HS, West Carrollton, OH
Lisa M. Fish
Shakopee HS, Shakopee, MN
Virginia Fizer
Pulaski County HS, Dublin, VA
Sandra Flettner
Fresno HS, Fresno, CA
Raoul Gabhart
West Craven HS, Vanceboro, NC
Ruben Garza
Crockett HS, Austin, TX
Raelene Gaskins,
West Craven HS, Vanceboro, NC
Lily Sans Grimes
Jones County HS, Gray, GA
Ronda Hall
Oklahoma Baptist Univ, Shawnee, OK
Rosa Hamilton
Sparta HS, Sparta, Wisconsin
Deana Hawkins
West Craven HS, Vanceboro, NC
Judy Hawkins
West Craven HS, Vanceboro, NC
Roger Hawkins
West Craven HS, Vanceboro, NC
Monica Hillard
Post Falls HS, Post Falls, ID
Charl Humphrey
West Craven HS, Vanceboro, NC
Dorothy LaCoste
Davis HS, Modesto, CA

Kathy LaHouze
Robinsdale Armstrong HS, Plymouth, MN
Robin Landress
Lynchburg Christian Acad, Lynchburg, VA
Erna Leach
Ada HS, Ada, OK
Becky Leek
Fort Scott HS, Fort Scott, KS
Pam Lessert
Ponca City HS, Ponca City, OK
R. Lael Littlefield
Marion HS, Marion, IN
Merinda Vinson McKinney
Mitchell HS, Bakersville, NC
Jan McDaniel
DeSoto HS, DeSoto, TX
Tanja M. Moore
Aiken HS, Aiken, NC
Ann Morris
Pike County HS, Zebulon, GA
Illona Morris
Putnam City North Sch, Oklahoma City, OK
Amiee Myatt
West Craven HS, Vanceboro, NC
Ruth A. Paulsen
Center HS, Kansas City, MO
Jennifer Peskie
West Craven HS, Vanceboro, NC
Nancy Pyle
John F. Kennedy HS, Suffolk, VA
Linda Reasonver
Gallatin HS, Gallatin, TN
Sherry Rowan
Mayfield Jr HS, Oklahoma City, OK
Shawn Sanders,
West Craven HS, Vanceboro, NC
Barbara Snyder
Burges HS, El Paso, TX
Martha L. Souza
Lawrence HS, Lawrence, KS
Donna Strawser,
Mt. Pleasant HS, Mt. Pleasant, TN
Brenda Watson
Madisonville-North Hopkins HS,
Madisonville, KY
Emily Westbrook
Checotah HS, Checotah, OK
Carol Wilson
Warren County R-III Sch, Warrenton, MO
Kay Zieghan
Richland Center HS, Richland Center, WI

FOREIGN FOOD TERMS

Al dente (Italian) - describes pasta which has been cooked just to the point at which it still offers a slight resistance to the teeth.

Antipasto (Italian) - appetizers, or dishes served "before the pasta".

Arroz (Spanish and Mexican) - any form of rice.

Au gratin (French) - describes a dish sprinkled with bread crumbs or cheese, and then baked.

Avgolemono (Greek) - a soup or sauce made from chicken stock, eggs and lemon.

Baklava (Greek and Turkish) - a dessert made of very thin sheets of pastry filled with nuts and honey, then baked. It is usually cut into diamond shapes.

Bisque (French) - a cream soup made with shellfish or purréed vegetables.

Borsch (Russian and Polish) - a beet soup, frequently containing other vegetables such as cabbage. It is served both hot or cold.

Brioche (French) - a slightly sweet bread usually served at breakfast.

Bulgur (Turkish and Lebanese) - parched and crushed wheat used as a dietary staple in Middle Eastern countries.

Chalupas (Mexican) - a spicy dish made with tortillas layered or filled with meat sauce and cheese.

Chutney (Indian) - a highly seasoned relish of fruits, herbs and spices.

Coquille (French) - literally, a shell; it refers to seafood dishes prepared in scallop shells or baking dishes in the shape of a shell. The best known dish is Coquilles St. Jacques, made with scallops.

Crêpe (French) - thin pancake, filled with sweet or savory mixtures, often served flaming or with a sauce.

Croutons (French) - small cubes of bread, often seasoned, served with soups or as garnish for salad.

Curry (East Indian) - any dish, including meat, fish, vegetables or fruit seasoned with curry powder.

Empanada (Mexican) - pastry filled with sweet or savory mixture. Frequently they take the form of turnovers and can be baked or fried.

Enchilada (Mexican) - rolled tortilla filled with meat or cheese and topped with chili sauce.

Feta (Greek) - soft white cheese made from the milk of goats or sheep and cured in brine.

Flan (Spanish) - a baked dessert custard.

Fondue (Swiss) - a hot dish, the main ingredient of which is melted cheese, into which pieces of bread are dipped. This version is the national dish of Switzerland. It can also refer to melted chocolate into which cake or fruit is dipped.

Gazpacho (Spanish) - a cold soup made with tomatoes and other fresh vegetables.

Jalapeño pepper (Mexican) - very hot small green pepper.

Lasagna (Italian) - a layered dish made with wide noodles, meat and cheese.

Leek - a root vegetable related to the onion.

Lentils (Near Eastern) - one of the oldest known legumes. Its flat seeds are always used dried and prepared like dried peas or beans.

Minestrone (Italian) - a soup made of fresh vegetables, dried beans and pasta.

Moussaka (Middle Eastern and Greek) - dish made of eggplant, onion and spices. It usually contains ground lamb as well.

Nougat (French and Italian) - a creamy sugar confection with nuts and/or fruit.

Paella (Spanish) - national dish of rice and any combination of seafood, chicken, sausage, vegetables and seasonings.

Pasta (Italian) - literally paste; it refers to noodle-like dough, either fresh or dried, which comes in over 100 different shapes and varieties such as spaghetti, macaroni, canneloni and rotini.

Pesto (Italian) - a green sauce made of basil, garlic, Parmesan cheese and pine nuts. It is served over pasta.

Phyllo (Greek and Middle Eastern) - tissue-thin layers of flaky pastry. The layers can be filled with sweet or savory mixtures and served as appetizer, main dish or dessert.

Pilaf (Middle Eastern) - rice dish which can include various combinations of meat, vegetables and seasonings. It can be served as a main dish or side dish.

Plantain (South American and African) - a starchy fruit similar to a banana and basic in the diet in the tropics. It is usually served cooked rather than fresh.

Quiche (French) - main dish one-crust pastry with savory custard filling.

Ratatouille (French) - a casserole or stew usually containing eggplant, zucchini, tomato and green pepper. It can include meat as well.

Salsa (Mexican) - a sauce containing tomatoes and green chili peppers.

Sangría (Spanish) - national drink of Spain; it usually includes red wine and various fruit juices.

Schnitzle (German) - a thin cutlet of pork or veal.

Seviche (South American) - appetizer or main dish of raw fish pickled or marinated in lime juice and mixed with onions and peppers.

Soufflé (French and Swiss) - a savory or sweet dish made with beaten eggs and baked until puffed.

Spätzle (German) - a very small dumpling made of flour.

Tortilla (Mexican) - the national bread of Mexico; it is a thin flat cake made of cornmeal or flour and baked on a griddle.

Tortoni (Italian) - a frozen dessert made with whipped cream, macaroon crumbs and liqueur.

Trifle (English) - a layered dessert made of custard, fruit and sponge cake spread with jam and soaked with spirits.

Vinaigrette (French) - a salad dressing named for its main ingredient, vinegar. It also includes oil, seasonings and herbs.

Yogurt (Near Eastern) - a milk product made acidic and thickened by the addition of bacterial cultures. It is a dietary staple in the Near East countries.

Zabaglione (Italian) - a dessert made of eggs, sugar and wine. It can be served warm or cold, alone or over fruit or cake.

HERBS AND SPICES

Allspice, a pungent, aromatic spice, comes whole or in powdered form. It is excellent in marinades, curries and desserts.

Anise, also known as fennel seed, has a slightly licorice flavor. It is used in cookies, cakes and pastries, as well as sauces.

Basil is a staple herb of Italian cooking, for it brings out the rich flavor of recipes calling for tomatoes. It is also good in cold poultry salads.

Bay leaf is the aromatic leaf of the laurel. It is the basis of the flavor in many French recipes, especially stews, soups, marinades and stuffings.

Cardamom is a member of the ginger family. It is used in Scandinavian and Indian cooking in pastries and curries.

Cayenne is a fiery hot powder made from dried peppers. It is used in Mexican and Indian cuisines in meat dishes and sauces.

Celery seed is from wild celery rather then domestic. It is especially good for seasoning bouillon or stock.

Chives, available fresh, dried or frozen, can be substituted for raw onion in almost any recipe.

Cinnamon, ground from the bark of the cinnamon tree is an important spice in desserts. It is also used in savory Indian and Indonesian dishes.

Clove is the flower bud of the clove tree. It can be used either whole or in powdered form with ham, soups and desserts.

Cumin is a staple spice in Mexican and Indian cooking. It comes as seeds and in powdered form.

Curry is used in Indian cooking. It is a combination of various spices, including allspice, cardomom, cayenne, cinnamon, coriander, cloves, cumin, fennel, ginger, mace, pepper and turmeric for color.

Dillweed is a member of the parsley family. It is used for pickling and in many German and Scandinavian dishes. It is particularly good in seafood and vegetable dishes.

Garlic, one of the oldest herbs of which there is a record, is used in Italian and Middle Eastern cooking. It should not be sautéed until it is too dark or the odor and taste become too strong.

Ginger is a pungent and spicy root. It is commonly used in Chinese and Indian cuisines for desserts, meats and vegetables.

Marjoram is an aromatic herb of the mint family. It is good in soups, sauces, stuffings and stews.

Mustard in powdered form is from ground mustard seeds. It brings a pleasant bite to sauces and enhances the flavor of roasted meat.

Nutmeg is a spice with a sweet and delicate flavor. It is frequently used in desserts, particularly fruit desserts. It lends a subtle flavor to meat and vegetable dishes as well.

Oregano is a member of the mint family with a biting and fragrant flavor. It is a staple herb in Italian, Spanish and Mexican cooking. It is very good in dishes with a tomato foundation.

Paprika, a mild pepper, adds color to many dishes, and it is especially flavorful in poultry recipes. The very best paprika is imported from Hungary where there are more than a dozen varieties, each with subtle differences in flavor.

Rosemary is an important seasoning in sauces and in stuffings for duck, partridge and capon.

Sage, the perennial favorite with all kinds of poultry, adds flavor or stuffings in particular. It is also good in hearty soups.

Savory is a member of the mint family. It is used with peas, beans, soups, stews and tomato juice.

Sesame seed should be toasted to bring out the nutty flavor. It is used on breads and in mildlly flavored meats and sauces. It is typical of African and Near Eastern cuisines.

Tarragon, one of the *fines herbes* in French cuisine, goes well with all poultry dishes except for soups. It is most frequently associated with Bearnaise sauce. It is also a good flavor for dressings for vegetable salads.

Thyme is used in combination with bay leaf in soups and stews. It is a popular herb in Spanish and Indian cooking.

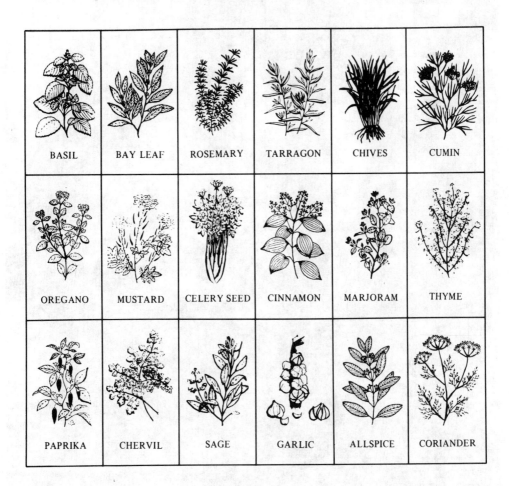

BASIL	BAY LEAF	ROSEMARY	TARRAGON	CHIVES	CUMIN
OREGANO	MUSTARD	CELERY SEED	CINNAMON	MARJORAM	THYME
PAPRIKA	CHERVIL	SAGE	GARLIC	ALLSPICE	CORIANDER

CUISINE FRANÇAISE

FRANCE

NEW CHICKEN SOUP

1 onion	1 bay leaf
2 cloves	1 sprig of thyme
4 carrots	Peppercorns to taste
3 stalks celery	5 3/4 cups water
1 turnip	Salt to taste
2 chicken breasts	7 ounces mushrooms

Stud onion with cloves. Combine onion, carrots, celery, turnip, chicken, bay leaf, thyme, peppercorns and water in saucepan. Bring to a boil. Season to taste with salt. Simmer for 30 minutes, skimming as necessary. Strain, reserving stock. Discard onion, thyme, bay leaf and peppercorns. Cut vegetables and chicken into thin slices. Add to stock. Trim and slice mushrooms. Add to soup. Simmer for 10 minutes. Yield: 4 servings.

NOUVELLE MARMITE AU POULET

1 oignon	1 feuille de laurier
2 clous de girofle	1 branche de thym
4 carottes	Poivre en grains
3 branches de céleri	1 1/2 litres d'eau
1 navet	Sel
2 blancs de poulet	200 grammes de champignons

Piquez l'oignon de clous de girofle. Mettez l'oignon, les carottes, le céleri, le navet, le poulet, une feuille de laurier, du thym, quelques grains de poivre et 1 litre 1/2 d'eau dans une marmite. Portez lentement à ébullition, salez et laisser cuire pendant 30 minutes en écumant de temps en temps. Passez le contenu de la marmite à travers une passoire fine. Recueillez le bouillon dans une casserole. Jetez l'oignon, le thym, le laurier et les grains de poivre. Coupez les légumes et les blancs de poulet en lamelles fines et remettez-les dans le bouillon dans la marmite. Coupez les champignons en tranches fines et ajoutez-les au bouillon. Laissez mijoter pendant 10 minutes.

LOBSTER BISQUE

2¹/2 cups chicken stock
1 onion, sliced
4 stalks celery, sliced
2 cloves
1 bay leaf
6 peppercorns

¹/4 cup butter
¹/4 cup flour
3 cups milk
2 cups chopped cooked lobster
1 cup hot cream

Combine chicken stock, onion, celery, cloves, bay leaf and peppercorns in saucepan. Simmer for 30 minutes. Strain, reserving stock. Melt butter in saucepan. Blend in flour. Add milk gradually. Cook until thickened, stirring constantly. Stir in lobster and reserved stock. Simmer for 5 minutes. Stir in hot cream at serving time. Do not boil. Garnish with paprika. Yield: 6 servings.

ONION SOUP (SOUPE À L'OIGNON)

1 pound yellow onions, sliced
¹/4 cup butter
2 tablespoons flour
4 cups water

5 beef bouillon cubes
¹/2 teaspoon salt
4 slices French bread, toasted
¹/2 cup Parmesan cheese

Sauté onions in butter in heavy saucepan. Stir in flour. Cook until flour is lightly browned. Reduce heat. Add water, bouillon and salt. Bring to a boil, stirring to dissolve bouillon. Simmer, covered, for 15 minutes. Ladle into oven-proof bowls. Top with French bread. Sprinkle with cheese. Broil until cheese is light brown. Yield: 4 servings.

POTATO SOUP (VICHYSSOISE)

3 medium leeks, minced
1 medium onion, minced
2 tablespoons butter
4 medium potatoes, peeled,
    sliced

4 cups chicken stock
1¹/2 cups cream
Salt and white pepper to taste

Sauté leeks and onion in butter in saucepan for 3 minutes. Add potatoes and chicken stock. Simmer, covered, for 15 minutes or until potatoes are tender. Place in blender or food processor container. Process until smooth. Stir in cream, salt and pepper. Chill until serving time or heat just to serving temperature in saucepan if preferred. Garnish with chives. Yield: 6 servings.

SAVORY HERBED BAKED BRIE

1 2-pound wheel Brie,
   8 inches in diameter
1 sheet frozen puff pastry
1/4 cup chopped parsley
1 clove of garlic, minced
1 teaspoon rosemary

1 teaspoon thyme
1 teaspoon marjoram
8 thin slices (2 ounces) hard
   salami, chopped
1 egg, lightly beaten

Place Brie in freezer for 30 minutes. Let pastry stand at room temperature for 20 minutes. Mix parsley, garlic and herbs in small bowl. Slice Brie into 2 layers. Spread herb mixture on bottom layer. Sprinkle with salami. Replace top layer. Unfold pastry sheet. Roll into 12 x 18-inch rectangle on floured surface. Place Brie in center of pastry. Bring up pastry to enclose Brie; cut off excess pastry. Brush edges with egg; press to seal. Place seam side down on lightly greased baking sheet. Brush with remaining egg. Cut 4 steam vents. Bake at 350° F. for 30 minutes or until pastry is golden and puffed. Let stand for 15 minutes. Serve with crackers. Yield: 15 to 20 servings.

Photograph for this recipe on Cover.

BRITTANY-STYLE SALAD

1 16-ounce can corn
1 16-ounce can crushed
   pineapple

1 large tomato
Vinaigrette salad dressing

Drain corn and pineapple. Chop tomato. Combine in large salad bowl. Add vinaigrette dressing to taste; mix well. Yield: 6 to 8 servings.

SALADE À LA BRETAGNE

1 boîte (16 onces) de maïs
1 boîte (16 onces) d'ananas,
   en morceaux ou écrasé

1 grande tomate
Sauce à la vinaigrette

Laissez égoutter le maïs et les ananas. Coupez la tomate en cubes. Mélangez tous dans un grand saladier. Arrosez le tout avec la sauce à la vinaigrette au goût.

BEAN SALAD VINAIGRETTE

1 pound fresh green beans
1 tomato, chopped
1 onion, chopped
3 tablespoons chopped parsley
2 teaspoons chopped capers

1 hard-boiled egg, chopped
1/2 cup vinegar and oil salad
    dressing
1 teaspoon mustard
Salt and pepper to taste

Cook green beans in water to cover in saucepan until tender-crisp; drain. Combine with tomato, onion, parsley, capers and egg in bowl. Combine remaining ingredients in small bowl. Add to salad; toss to mix well. Chill until serving time. Serve in lettuce-lined salad bowl. Yield: 4 to 6 servings.

SALADE NIÇOISE

1 9-ounce package frozen
    artichoke hearts
2 hard-boiled eggs, sliced
1 7-ounce can tuna, drained,
    flaked
2 cups chopped cooked
    potatoes
1 head lettuce, torn

1/2 cup chopped celery
1/2 cup chopped green pepper
2 tomatoes, cut into wedges
2/3 cup olive oil
1/3 cup red wine vinegar
1 tablespoon prepared mustard
1/2 teaspoon salt
Ground pepper to taste

Cook artichoke hearts according to package directions; drain. Combine with eggs, tuna and vegetables in large salad bowl. Mix olive oil, vinegar, mustard, salt and pepper in small bowl. Add to salad; toss lightly to mix. Garnish with black olives and anchovies. Yield: 10 servings.

TOMATO SALAD (SALADE DE TOMATES)

4 ripe tomatoes
2 heads endive
1 tablespoon chopped parsley
1 tablespoon chopped chives

1 tablespoon basil
3 tablespoons olive oil
1 tablespoon vinegar
Salt and pepper to taste

Place tomatoes in boiling water for 1 or 2 seconds. Remove skin and cut into thin slices. Arrange endive leaves on serving plate. Arrange tomato slices on endive. Sprinkle with herbs. Mix olive oil and vinegar in small bowl. Drizzle over salad. Season to taste. Yield: 6 servings.

BEEF BURGUNDY

3 ounces bacon, chopped	1 clove of garlic, minced
10 to 15 small onions	1/4 teaspoon thyme
2 pounds lean beef, cubed	1 bay leaf
Salt and pepper to taste	2 cups Burgundy
1 tablespoon flour	1 cup bouillon

Fry bacon in heavy saucepan until crisp. Remove with slotted spoon. Sauté onions in drippings in saucepan. Add beef. Season to taste. Sprinkle flour over beef. Cook for several minutes, stirring constantly. Add garlic, thyme, bay leaf, wine and bouillon. Simmer, covered, for 2 hours. Yield: 6 servings.

BOEUF BOURGUIGNON

250 grammes de lard ou poitrine fumée	1 cuillerée à soupe de farine
10 à 15 petits oignons, entiers	1 gousse d'ail
1 kilogramme de boeuf maigre, coupé en cubes	1/4 cuillerée à café de thym
	1 feuille de laurier
Sel et poivre	1/2 litre de vin rouge
	1/4 litre de bouillon de boeuf

Faites revenir doucement au saindoux le lard ou la poitrine fumée coupé en dés ainsi que les petits oignons. Quand le tout est bien doré, ajoutez le boeuf maigre. Assaisonnez. Saupoudrez d'une cuillerée de farine. Remuez. Ajoutez l'ail, le thym et la feuille de laurier. Mouillez avec le vin et le bouillon. Couvrez hermétiquement et laissez mijoter pendant environ 2 heures.

PEPPER STEAK (STEAK AU POIVRE)

8 peppercorns	1/2 cup bouillon or red wine
4 sirloin steaks	

Crush peppercorns with rolling pin. Press onto both sides of steaks. Let stand for 10 minutes. Heat oiled skillet until very hot. Add steaks. Sear well on both sides; reduce heat to medium. Cook steaks to desired degree of doneness. Remove to serving platter. Stir bouillon or wine into skillet, stirring to deglaze. Spoon over steaks. May use minute steaks for an economical substitute. Yield: 4 servings.

CHICKEN MARENGO (POULET MARENGO)

1 chicken, cut up	1 large onion, chopped
Flour	1 clove of garlic, minced
Salt	2/3 cup dry white wine
2 tablespoons butter	1 tablespoon tomato paste
2 tablespoons olive oil	8 ounces mushrooms

Roll chicken pieces in flour seasoned with salt, coating well. Brown chicken on all sides in mixture of butter and olive oil in saucepan. Add onion and garlic. Sauté for 2 minutes. Stir in wine. Simmer for 3 minutes. Add tomato paste and enough water to make a thin sauce without covering chicken. Simmer, covered, for 30 minutes. Add mushrooms. Simmer for 10 minutes. Arrange chicken on serving platter. Pour sauce over chicken. Garnish with parsley.
Yield: 4 to 5 servings.

CHICKEN IN WINE (COQ AU VIN)

1 chicken, cut up	1 1/2 cups water
2 tablespoons bacon drippings	8 ounces mushrooms, cut into
Salt and pepper to taste	quarters
3 cups dry red wine	1 tablespoon oil
2 cups bouillon	2 tablespoons melted margarine
20 small onions	3 tablespoons flour
2 tablespoons oil	

Brown chicken in bacon drippings in saucepan. Season to taste. Add wine and bouillon. Simmer for 30 minutes. Place onions in boiling water to cover in saucepan. Cook for 1 minute; drain well. Sauté onions in 2 tablespoons oil in small saucepan until light brown. Add 1 1/2 cups water and seasonings to taste. Simmer for 30 minutes. Sauté mushrooms in 1 tablespoon oil in skillet until golden. Blend margarine and flour in saucepan. Cook for several minutes. Drain chicken, reserving 2 1/2 cups broth. Stir reserved broth into flour mixture gradually. Cook until thickened, stirring constantly. Add onions, mushrooms and chicken. Heat to serving temperature. Yield: 4 to 5 servings.

COQUILLES ST. JACQUES

Parsley, celery, thyme and bay
  leaf to taste
1¹/4 pounds sea scallops
6 shallots, chopped
2 tablespoons butter
1¹/2 cups dry white wine
Salt to taste
12 mushrooms
2 tablespoons butter
¹/3 cup water

Juice of 1 lemon
¹/2 teaspoon salt
Pepper to taste
3 tablespoons melted butter
3 tablespoons flour
4 egg yolks
1 cup heavy cream
Parmesan cheese
Fine dry bread crumbs

Tie parsley, celery, thyme and bay leaf in cheesecloth. Combine with scallops, shallots, 2 tablespoons butter and wine in saucepan. Season with salt to taste. Simmer for 5 minutes or just until scallops are tender. Drain, reserving broth. Discard bag of seasonings. Cool scallops. Slice thinly. Sauté mushrooms in 2 tablespoons butter for 2 to 3 minutes. Add ¹/3 cup water, lemon juice, ¹/2 teaspoon salt and pepper to taste. Simmer for several minutes or until mushrooms are tender. Drain, reserving liquid. Blend 3 tablespoons butter and flour in saucepan. Stir in reserved liquids from scallops and mushrooms. Cook until thickened and smooth, stirring constantly. Add scallops. Cook until heated through. Beat egg yolks with cream in bowl. Add to sauce very gradually, stirring constantly until thickened. Do not boil. Add mushrooms. Spoon into individual ramekins or shells. Sprinkle with cheese and crumbs. Broil just until light brown.
Yield: 6 servings.

SEAFOOD QUICHE

¹/2 cup chopped onion
1 teaspoon oil
8 ounces seafood
1 cup cubed Cheddar cheese
1 unbaked 9-inch pie shell

3 eggs, lightly beaten
1 large can evaporated milk
¹/4 teaspoon nutmeg
¹/2 teaspoon salt
¹/4 teaspoon pepper

Sauté onion in oil in skillet until transparent. Layer onion, seafood and cheese in pie shell. Combine eggs, evaporated milk and seasonings in bowl; mix well. Pour into pie shell. Bake at 450° F. for 15 minutes. Reduce temperature to 350° F. Bake for 10 to 20 minutes or until knife inserted in center comes out clean.
Yield: 6 to 8 servings.

EGGS AND SHRIMP AU GRATIN

6 eggs
1 tablespoon butter
1 tablespoon chopped parsley
1 tablespoon prepared French
   mustard

1/4 pound peeled cooked
   shrimp
2 cups cream
Salt and pepper to taste
1/2 cup shredded cheese

Boil eggs in water in saucepan for 8 minutes. Place in cold water for 2 minutes. Peel eggs. Slice into baking dish. Add butter, parsley, mustard, chopped shrimp, cream and salt and pepper to taste. Sprinkle with cheese. Bake at 400° F. for 15 to 20 minutes. Yield: 6 servings.

OEUFS DURS GRATINÉS AU FROMAGE

6 oeufs
1 cuillerée à soupe de beurre
1 cuillerée à soupe de persil
1 cuillerée à soupe de
   moutarde forte

125 grammes de crevettes,
   bouillies et décortiquées
2 tasses de crème
Sel et poivre
1/2 tasse de fromage râpé

Laissez bouiller les oeufs dans une casserole pendant 8 minutes pour qu'ils durcissent. Plongez-les dans de l'eau froide pendant 2 minutes. Retirez-les coquilles. Coupez-les en tranches dans une petite casserole. Ajoutez le beurre, le persil, la moutarde, les crevettes hachées, la crème et un peu de sel et de poivre. Saupoudrez avec le fromage. Faites gratiner dans un four à 400° F. pendant 15 à 20 minutes.

SOLE WITH ALMONDS (SOLE AMANDINE)

2 pounds sole fillets
1/4 cup flour
1 tablespoon paprika
1 teaspoon salt
2 tablespoons oil

1/4 cup butter
2 tablespoons lemon juice
1/4 teaspoon Tabasco sauce
1/2 cup toasted slivered
   almonds

Roll fish in mixture of flour, paprika and salt, coating well. Place in greased broiler pan. Brush with oil. Broil for 5 to 8 minutes or until a golden crust forms; do not turn. Remove to heated platter. Melt butter in saucepan. Add lemon juice and Tabasco sauce. Pour over fish. Sprinkle with almonds. Yield: 4 servings.

HAM WITH CIDER

2 onions	3 tablespoons butter
5 tablespoons butter	2 tablespoons parsley
1 large slice country ham,	3/4 teaspoon thyme
1 inch thick, boned	2$1/2$ cups cider

Peel and chop onions. Melt 5 tablespoons butter in skillet. Add onions. Cook until transparent. Brown ham lightly in 3 tablespoons butter in skillet. Place ham in baking dish. Add onions, parsley, thyme and cider. Bake at 225° F. for 45 minutes. Yield: 4 servings.

JAMBON AU CIDRE

500 grammes d'oignons	50 grammes de beurre
75 grammes de beurre	2 cuillerées à soupe de persil
1 belle tranche de jambon de	3/4 cuillerée à café de thym
pays, désossé	2$1/2$ tasses de cidre

Épluchez et éminez les oignons. Faites chauffer dans une poêle 75 grammes de beurre. Mettez-y les oignons et faites cuire doucement. Faites revenir le jambon dans 50 grammes de beurre fondu dans une autre poêle. Mettez le jambon dans un plat allant au four. Ajoutez les oignons, du persil, du thym et le cidre. Faites cuire au four à 225° F. pendant 45 minutes.

COUNTRY TART (TOURTE DE CAMPAGNE)

2 sheets frozen puff pastry,	2 stalks celery, chopped
thawed	5 shallots, chopped
2 eggs	5 tablespoons chopped parsley
8 ounces chopped cooked ham	2 tomatoes, chopped
1 leek, chopped	Salt and pepper to taste
1 carrot, chopped	

Roll 1 sheet pastry thin on floured surface. Place on greased baking sheet. Beat eggs in bowl. Spoon into greased small skillet. Cook until partially set. Stir in ham, leek, carrot, celery, shallots, parsley, tomatoes, salt and pepper. Spoon onto pastry. Roll remaining sheet pastry on floured surface. Place over filling. Seal edges; cut steam vents. Bake at 350° F. for 40 minutes or until brown.
Yield: 6 servings.

EGG AND HAM SOUFFLÉ

1/4 cup dry bread crumbs
1 cup warm milk
3 hard-boiled eggs
3 eggs, separated

2 tablespoons melted butter
1/4 cup chopped cooked ham
Nutmeg, salt, pepper to taste
2 tablespoons butter

Soak bread crumbs in milk in bowl; mix to a thick paste. Cut boiled eggs into quarters. Arrange whites in star pattern in buttered 1-quart soufflé dish. Mash cooked yolks with bread mixture. Add uncooked egg yolks; mix well. Add melted butter and ham. Season to taste with nutmeg, salt and pepper. Beat egg whites in bowl until stiff peaks form. Fold gently into ham mixture. Spoon into prepared soufflé dish. Dot with 2 tablespoons butter. Bake at 425° F. for 15 to 20 minutes or until golden brown. Serve immediately. Yield: 4 servings.

CHEESE SOUFFLÉ (SOUFFLÉ AU FROMAGE)

2 tablespoons butter
2 tablespoons flour
1 1/2 cups milk
3 egg yolks
1 teaspoon salt

1 1/2 cups shredded Cheddar
  cheese
1/2 cup chopped chives
5 egg whites, stiffly beaten

Melt butter in saucepan. Heat until butter stops foaming. Blend in flour. Add milk gradually. Cook until thickened, stirring constantly. Remove from heat. Beat in egg yolks 1 at a time. Add salt. Reserve 1 tablespoon cheese. Add remaining cheese and chives to milk mixture; mix well. Fold in stiffly beaten egg whites. Spoon into buttered 6-cup soufflé dish. Sprinkle with reserved cheese. Bake at 400° F. for 30 to 35 minutes or until golden brown. Yield: 4 to 6 servings.

QUICHE LORRAINE

4 eggs
1 1/2 cups milk
2 cups shredded Swiss cheese
8 slices bacon, crisp-fried,
  crumbled

1 teaspoon chopped chives
1/2 teaspoon salt
1/4 teaspoon pepper
1 unbaked 9-inch pie shell
Nutmeg

Beat eggs in bowl. Add milk, cheese, bacon, chives, salt and pepper. Pour into pie shell. Sprinkle with nutmeg. Bake at 400° F. for 30 to 35 minutes or until knife inserted in center comes out clean. Yield: 6 servings.

ASPARAGUS WITH HOLLANDAISE SAUCE
(ASPERGES HOLLANDAISE)

1 pound asparagus
2 egg yolks
1 cup butter

1 to 2 teaspoons lemon juice
Salt to taste

Cut off tough lower stems of asparagus. Cook in salted boiling water in saucepan just until tender; drain. Place on serving plate. Beat egg yolks in top of double boiler until thick and lemon-colored. Place over hot but not boiling water. Add butter very gradually, stirring constantly. Stir in lemon juice and salt. Spoon a small amount over asparagus. Pour remaining sauce into serving dish. Serve with asparagus. Yield: 4 servings.

BEETS IN SPICY SAUCE

1 pound beets, cooked
1 cup sour cream
1 teaspoon Dijon mustard

1 tablespoon catsup
Salt and pepper to taste

Peel beets. Cut into small dice. Combine cream, mustard, catsup, salt and pepper in bowl. Add beets; mix well. Chill until serving time. Yield: 4 servings.

BETTERAVES À LA SAUCE DIABLE

400 grammes de betteraves
   rouges, cuites
1 tasse de crème fraîche
1 cuillerée à café de moutarde
   forte

1 cuillerée à soupe de sauce
   tomate
Sel et poivre

Épluchez les betteraves. Coupez-les en petits dés. Mélangez la créme fraîche, la moutarde, la sauce tomate, le sel et le poivre dans un bol. Ajoutez les betteraves; mélangez bien. Servez frais.

BRAISED CELERY (CÉLERIS BRAISÉS)

2 small bunches celery
1¼ cups chicken bouillon

⅓ cup butter
Salt and pepper to taste

Cut celery into 2-inch pieces. Combine with bouillon in saucepan. Simmer just until tender-crisp. Drain, reserving cooking liquid. Add butter to celery in saucepan. Cook until celery is lightly browned. Season to taste. Stir in a small amount of reserved cooking liquid. Cook until reduced to desired consistency. Yield: 6 servings.

POTATO AND EGG PIE (PÂTÉ AUX OEUFS)

4 medium potatoes, peeled,
  chopped
2 tablespoons butter
¼ cup heavy cream
Salt, pepper and nutmeg to
  taste
2 tablespoons melted butter

2 tablespoons flour
2 cups milk
White pepper to taste
5 hard-boiled eggs, sliced
2 tablespoons chopped fresh
  parsley
1 egg, beaten

Cook potatoes in water in saucepan until tender; drain. Mash potatoes with 2 tablespoons butter, cream, salt, pepper and nutmeg in bowl. Blend 2 tablespoons melted butter and flour in heavy saucepan. Cook over low heat for 2 to 5 minutes, stirring constantly. Whisk in milk. Season lightly with salt. Cook over low heat until thickened to desired consistency. Add white pepper and nutmeg to taste. Alternate layers of mashed potatoes, sliced eggs, parsley and white sauce in buttered 1½-quart baking dish until all ingredients are used, ending with potatoes. Smooth top with wet knife. Brush with beaten egg. Bake at 350° F. for 30 minutes or until lightly browned. Yield: 6 servings.

RATATOUILLE

3/4 cup thinly sliced onion
2 cloves of garlic, chopped
1/3 cup olive oil
4 green peppers, julienned
2 1/2 cups chopped peeled
 eggplant

3 cups sliced zucchini
2 cups chopped peeled
 tomatoes
Salt and pepper to taste
Olive oil

Sauté onion and garlic in 1/3 cup olive in heavy saucepan until golden. Add layers of remaining vegetables, seasoning each layer to taste. Sprinkle with a small amount of additional olive oil. Simmer, covered, over low heat for 40 minutes. Simmer, uncovered, for 10 minutes or until liquid is reduced to desired consistency. Serve hot or cold. Yield: 6 to 8 servings.

TOMATOES PROVENÇALE

4 firm ripe tomatoes
2 tablespoons oil
2 cloves of garlic, minced
1/4 cup minced parsley

1/4 cup fine dry bread crumbs
Salt to taste
Butter

Slice unpeeled tomatoes into halves through stem ends. Sauté cut side down in oil in skillet over low heat until tender. Turn tomatoes over. Cook for 1 minute. Place cut side up in greased shallow oven-proof dish; keep warm. Cook garlic and parsley in pan juices for 2 to 3 minutes. Stir in crumbs and salt to taste. Spoon crumb mixture onto tomatoes. Dot with butter. Broil until crumbs are brown. Yield: 4 servings.

GARLIC BREAD

8 slices French bread
1/2 cup butter, softened
2 teaspoons garlic powder

1 teaspoon pepper
2 tablespoons Romano Cheese
Parsley flakes

Spread bread with butter. Place on baking sheet. Sprinkle with garlic powder, pepper, cheese and parsley. Broil until light brown. Yield: 8 servings.

BRIOCHE

1/2 cup milk	1/2 teaspoon salt
1/3 cup butter	1 cup flour
1 package yeast	2 eggs
2 tablespoons lukewarm water	1 cup flour
1/4 cup sugar	

Scald milk in saucepan. Stir in butter. Cool to lukewarm. Dissolve yeast in lukewarm water. Combine milk, yeast, sugar, salt and 1 cup flour in bowl. Add eggs; mix well. Mix in remaining 1 cup flour. Chill in refrigerator overnight. Knead on lightly floured surface until smooth. Divide into 2 portions. Shape each portion into 9 balls. Place 16 balls in greased fluted brioche cups. Shape remaining dough into 16 small balls. Place 1 in shallow cut on top of each roll. Let rise, covered, in warm place until doubled in bulk. Bake at 450° F. for 10 minutes. Yield: 16 rolls.

FRENCH BREAD

1/2 cup milk	1 tablespoon sugar
1 cup boiling water	4 cups flour
1 package yeast	2 teaspoons sugar
1/4 cup lukewarm water	2 teaspoons salt
1 1/2 tablespoons shortening	

Scald milk in saucepan. Add 1 cup boiling water. Cool to lukewarm. Dissolve yeast in 1/4 cup lukewarm water. Let stand for 10 minutes. Add yeast mixture, shortening and 1 tablespoon sugar to milk. Combine flour, 2 teaspoons sugar and salt in bowl; make well in center. Pour in milk mixture; mix to form a soft dough. Do not knead. Let rise, covered, in warm place for 2 hours or until doubled in bulk. Punch dough down. Divide into 2 portions. Pat into 2 rectangles on floured surface. Roll into 2 long French loaves. Place on greased baking sheet. Slash tops diagonally. Let rise until almost doubled in bulk. Bake at 400° F. for 15 minutes. Reduce temperature to 350°. Bake for 30 minutes longer. Yield: 2 loaves.

BLENDER CRÊPES

2¹/4 cups milk
4 eggs
2 cups flour

¹/4 cup oil
¹/4 teaspoon salt

Combine all ingredients in blender container; process until smooth. Heat greased nonstick 7-inch crêpe pan over medium heat. Pour 2 tablespoons batter into pan, tilting to coat well. Bake for 30 seconds or until lightly browned on bottom. Turn crêpe. Cook for 30 seconds longer. Repeat process with remaining batter. Fill as desired. Yield: 2 dozen.

CRÊPES FRANGIPANE

³/4 cup flour
¹/4 teaspoon salt
3 eggs
1 cup milk

3 tablespoons melted butter
2 tablespoons melted butter
Confectioners' sugar

Combine flour, salt, eggs, milk and 3 tablespoons butter in mixer bowl; beat until smooth. Heat lightly buttered 8-inch crêpe pan over medium heat. Pour 2 to 3 tablespoons batter into pan, rotating pan to coat well. Bake over medium heat until lightly browned on both sides. Repeat process with remaining batter. Spread scant 3 tablespoons Almond Cream Filling on each crêpe. Fold into halves, then into quarters. Arrange in shallow baking pan. Brush with 2 tablespoons melted butter. Bake at 350° F. for 10 minutes or just until heated through. Sprinkle with confectioners' sugar. Serve warm with whipped cream and chocolate curls. Yield: 12 crêpes.

Almond Cream Filling

³/4 cup sugar
¹/4 cup flour
1 cup milk
2 eggs
2 egg yolks

3 tablespoons butter
¹/2 cup ground almonds
1 teaspoon vanilla extract
¹/2 teaspoon almond extract

Mix sugar and flour in saucepan. Add milk gradually. Bring to a boil, stirring constantly. Cook for 1 minute. Beat eggs and egg yolks in bowl. Stir a small amount of hot mixture into eggs; stir eggs into hot mixture. Cook over low heat for 1 minute, stirring constantly; do not boil. Remove from heat. Stir in remaining ingredients. Cool.

Photograph for this recipe on page 10.

BÛCHE DE NOËL

3 to 6 egg yolks
1/2 cup confectioners' sugar
1 teaspoon vanilla extract
4 to 6 tablespoons baking
  cocoa
1/8 teaspoon salt
3 to 6 egg whites
1/2 teaspoon cream of tartar
1 cup whipping cream

Sugar to taste
2 ounces unsweetened baking
  chocolate
2 tablespoons butter
1/4 cup hot water
1/8 teaspoon salt
2 cups confectioners' sugar
1 teaspoon vanilla extract
1/2 chopped nuts (optional)

Beat egg yolks in bowl until light. Sift in 1/2 cup confectioners' sugar, beating until thick and lemon-colored. Add 1 teaspoon vanilla and sifted mixture of cocoa and 1/8 teaspoon salt; mix well. Beat egg whites in bowl until frothy. Add cream of tartar. Beat until stiff but not dry. Fold gently into batter. Spread in greased 10 x 15-inch cake pan lined with greased foil. Bake at 350° F. for 25 minutes. Cool in pan for 5 minutes. Invert onto towel sprinkled with confectioners' sugar. Remove foil; trim dry edges. Roll cake up in towel. Cool. Whip cream with sugar to taste in bowl until soft peaks form. Unroll cake. Spread with whipped cream. Roll as for jelly roll. Place seam side down on serving plate. Melt unsweetened chocolate and 2 tablespoons butter in saucepan; blend well. Remove from heat. Stir in hot water and 1/8 teaspoon salt. Add remaining ingredients gradually, mixing well. Spread on cake; mark to resemble log. Yield: 8 to 10 servings.

CHOCOLATE GÂTEAU

2/3 cup butter, softened
3/4 cup sugar
3 egg yolks
5 ounces semisweet baking
  chocolate, melted
2/3 cup flour
1/4 cup milk
1/2 cup ground almonds
1/2 teaspoon vanilla extract

3 egg whites
1/2 teaspoon salt
5 ounces semisweet baking
  chocolate
1/4 cup butter
3 tablespoons milk
1 cup confectioners' sugar
1/4 teaspoon almond extract
1/2 cup ground almonds

Cream 2/3 cup butter in mixer bowl until light. Add sugar 2 tablespoons at a time, beating until fluffy. Blend in egg yolks and 5 ounces melted chocolate. Add flour alternately with 1/4 cup milk, beginning and ending with flour and mixing well at low speed after each addition. Mix in 1/2 cup almonds and vanilla. Beat egg whites with salt in mixer bowl until stiff peaks form. Fold gently into batter. Spoon into lightly greased 9-inch springform pan. Bake at 350° F. for 25 to 30 minutes or until cake tests done. Cool in pan for 10 minutes. Remove to wire rack to cool completely. Melt 5 ounces chocolate with 1/4 cup butter and 3 tablespoons milk in double boiler. Remove from heat. Add confectioners' sugar and almond extract; beat until smooth. Spread over top and side of cake. Sprinkle top with 1/2 cup ground almonds. Garnish with sliced almonds. Yield: 12 servings.

CHOCOLATE FONDUE

2 tablespoons honey
1/2 cup half and half
1   9-ounce bar chocolate,
    broken into pieces

1 teaspoon vanilla extract
1/4 cup chopped toasted
    almonds

Heat honey and half and half in fondue pot over direct heat. Reduce heat. Add chocolate pieces. Heat until chocolate is melted, stirring constantly. Add the vanilla and almonds. Serve with pieces of cake, apple slices, strawberries or marshmallows. Yield: 8 servings.

FONDUE AU CHOCOLAT

2 cuillerées à soupe de miel
1 demi-tasse de crème légère
1 tablette (9-onces) de
    chocolat cassée en petits
    morceaux

1 cuillerées à café de vanille
1/4 tasse d'amandes grillées

Chaffez le miel et la crème dans un caquelon sur grande chaleur directe. Baissez la chaleur. Ajoutez les morceaux de chocolat. Chauffez, en remuant constamment, jusqu'à ce que tout le chocolat soit fondu. Ajoutez la vanille et les amandes. Servez avec des morceaux de gâteau, des tranches de pommes, des tranches de bananes, des fraises ou des pâtes de guimauve.

CHOCOLATE POTS DE CRÈME

1¹/₂ cups heavy cream
6 ounces chocolate chips
¹/₄ cup sugar

Salt to taste
4 egg yolks, beaten
2 teaspoons grated orange rind

Combine cream, chocolate chips, sugar and salt in 4-cup measure. Microwave, tightly covered with SARAN WRAP™, turning back edge to vent, on High for 4 minutes or until chocolate is melted, stirring twice. Add egg yolks, beating just until mixed. Microwave, covered, leaving vent, on Medium for 1¹/₂ minutes, stirring twice. Stir in orange rind. Pour into dessert dishes. Chill until serving time. Garnish with sweetened whipped cream. Yield: 4 servings.

Photograph for this recipe on Cover.

CHOCOLATE TRUFFLES

6 ounces semisweet baking
   chocolate
10 tablespoons butter, softened
2 egg yolks, beaten

1¹/₂ cups sifted confectioners'
   sugar
2 teaspoons vanilla extract
Cocoa

Melt chocolate in saucepan over very low heat, stirring constantly. Cool. Cream butter with egg yolks in bowl. Add confectioners' sugar gradually, blending well. Stir in chocolate and vanilla. Chill until firm enough to handle. Shape into 30 to 35 balls. Roll in cocoa. Store in airtight container. Yield: 30 to 35 truffles.

TRUFFES AU CHOCOLAT

6 onces de chocolat demi-sucré
10 cuillerées à soupe de
   beurre, ramolli
2 jaunes d'oeuf, battus

1¹/₂ tasses de sucre glace
2 cuillerées à café de vanille
Du cacao

Faites fondre le chocolat dans une casserole sur un feu très doux en remuant constamment. Faites refroidir. Mélangez dans un bol le beurre avec les jaunes d'oeuf. Ajoutez petit à petit le sucre; mélangez bien. Ajoutez le chocolat et la vanille. Mettez au réfrigérator jusqûa ce que le mélange soit ferme. Formez en 30 à 35 boules. Roulez dans du cacao. Conservez dans un récipient bien fermé.

FLOATING ISLANDS (OEUFS À LA NEIGE)

10 egg whites
1/4 teaspoon cream of tartar
Pinch of salt
1 cup confectioners' sugar
4 cups milk
1 cup sugar

10 egg yolks
1/4 cup milk
1 teaspoon vanilla extract
2 teaspoons confectioners'
  sugar

Beat egg whites, cream of tartar and salt in large mixer bowl until soft peaks form. Add 1 cup confectioners' sugar very gradually, beating constantly until stiff but not dry peaks form. Combine 4 cups milk and sugar in 12-inch skillet. Bring just to the simmering point over medium heat, stirring to dissolve sugar completely. Scoop meringue into islands with 2 large spoons. Slide carefully into milk. Cook 5 or 6 at a time for 1 minute on each side. Do not overcook. Place 1 inch apart on baking sheet. Chill in refrigerator. Blend egg yolks with 1/4 cup milk in double boiler. Stir in warm milk from skillet. Cook over simmering water for 15 to 20 minutes or until mixture coats spoon, stirring constantly. Stir in vanilla. Place pan in bowl of ice until well chilled. Spoon custard into serving bowl or individual serving dishes. Sprinkle meringues lightly with 2 teaspoons confectioners' sugar. Broil for 15 to 20 seconds or just until lightly browned. Place meringues on custard with slotted spoon. Chill, covered, for several hours to overnight. Serve with fresh fruit if desired. Yield: 10 servings.

PEARS À LA CRÈME

2 tablespoons butter
1/3 cup packed brown sugar
1/2 teaspoon cinnamon
1/4 teaspoon ginger

1 29-ounce can pear halves,
  drained
Vanilla ice cream

Combine butter, brown sugar, cinnamon and ginger in saucepan. Bring to a simmer, stirring to mix well. Add pears. Simmer for 10 minutes, turning once. Spoon ice cream into dessert dishes. Top with pears and syrup. Serve immediately. May substitute peaches for pears. Yield: 4 servings.

DEUTSCHE KÜCHE

GERMANY

FRUIT PUNCH

3/4 cup (or more) sugar
2 pounds strawberries,
    chopped peaches or chopped
    pineapple
2 quarts apple juice, chilled

Juice of 2 lemons
1 quart cranberry juice or
    Johannisbeersaft, chilled
1 quart soda water, chilled

Sprinkle sugar over fruit in bowl. Add a small amount of apple juice. Chill in refrigerator for several hours. Combine with remaining apple juice, lemon juice, cranberry juice and soda in punch bowl; mix gently. Yield: 20 to 24 servings.

ALKOHOLFREIE BOWLE

150 Gramm (oder mehr)
    Zucker
2 Pfund Erdbeeren oder in
    Stückchen geschnittene
    Pfirsiche oder Ananas
2 Liter Apfelsaft, kalt gestellt

Saft von 2 Zitronen
1 Liter Preiselbeersaft oder
    Johannisbeersaft, kalt gestellt
1 Liter Selterswasser, kalt
    gestellt

Den Zucker über das Obst in einer Schüssel streuen. Mit etwas Apfelsaft begießen. Einige Stunden im Kühlschrank kalt stellen. Dann den restlichen Apfelsaft, Zitronensaft, Preiselbeersaft und das Selterswasser zusammen mit dem Obstgemisch in eine Punschbowle geben; vorsichtig unterrühren.

CHEESE BALLS (KÄSETRÜFFEL)

6 tablespoons butter, softened
8 ounces cream cheese,
    softened
2 teaspoons sour cream

2 teaspoons sugar
Fine dark pumpernickel bread
    crumbs

Cream butter and cream cheese in mixer bowl until smooth. Add sour cream and sugar; mix well. Chill in refrigerator. Shape into balls. Roll in bread crumbs. Place in bonbon cups. Chill until serving time. Yield: 4 servings.

HOT BEER SOUP

1/2 cup sugar	1/3 cup sour cream
3 12-ounce bottles of	1/2 teaspoon cinnamon
reduced-calorie beer	1/2 teaspoon salt
4 egg yolks	Freshly ground pepper to taste

Bring sugar and beer to a boil in heavy 4-quart saucepan, stirring until sugar is dissolved. Remove from heat. Beat egg yolks with wire whisk in bowl. Blend in sour cream gradually. Stir 1/4 cup hot mixture into egg yolks; stir egg yolks into hot mixture. Add seasonings. Cook over low heat until mixture thickens slightly, stirring constantly; do not boil. Ladle into soup bowls. Yield: 4 servings.

HEIßE BIERSUPPE

100 Gramm Zucker	1/2 Teelöffel Zimt
1 Liter kaloriearmes Bier (3	1/4 Teelöffel Salz
Flaschen zu je 12 Unzen)	Frisch gemahlener Pfeffer
4 Eigelb	nach Geschmack
1/4 Tasse saure Sahne	

Den Zucker und das Bier in einem 4 Liter großen, schweren Topf zum Kochen bringen, verrühren, bis der Zucker aufgelöst ist. Vom Herd nehmen. Die Eigelb in einer kleinen Schüssel verquirlen, und die Sahne langsam darunter geben. 1/4 Tasse heißes Bier in das Eigelb-Sahnegemisch geben, dann das Gemisch in das heiße Bier schütten. Die Gewürze hinzugeben. Über niedriger Hitze erwärmen, bis das Gemisch leicht gedickt wird; nicht kochen. Die Suppe in Suppenschüsseln servieren.

CHERRY SOUP

1 pound cherries	2 tablespoons sugar
8 cups water	Juice of 1/2 lemon
1/4 cup tapioca	Grated lemon rind to taste

Combine cherries with water in saucepan. Cook until cherries are tender. Drain, reserving liquid. Press cherries through fine strainer. Combine pulp with reserved liquid in saucepan. Stir in tapioca. Cook until transparent, stirring constantly. Add sugar, lemon juice and lemon rind. Chill until serving time. Ladle into soup bowls. Garnish with fresh fruit. Yield: 4 to 6 servings.

SPLIT PEA SOUP

1 pound dried split green peas
1 meaty ham bone
3 large carrots, coarsely
  chopped
3 stalks celery, coarsely
  chopped
1 large unpeeled onion,
  coarsely chopped

1 teaspoon sage
2 teaspoons salt
1 teaspoon pepper
8 cups water
1/3 cup finely chopped carrots
1/3 cup finely chopped celery
1/3 cup finely chopped onion

Combine peas with enough water to cover by 2 inches in bowl. Let stand overnight. Bring ham bone, coarsely chopped vegetables, seasonings and 8 cups water to a boil in large saucepan. Reduce heat. Simmer for 3 hours, stirring occasionally. Strain, reserving stock and ham bone. Drain peas. Combine peas with 4 cups reserved stock in saucepan. Simmer for 3 hours. Add ham cut from bone and finely chopped vegetables. Add additional stock if necessary for desired consistency. Simmer for 1 hour. Yield: 6 to 8 servings.

ERBENSUPPE

1 Pfund trockene Erbsen
1 Schinkenknochen mit etwas
  Fleisch daran
3 große Karrotten, grob
  zerschnitten
3 Selleriestangen, grob
  zerschnitten
1 große, ungeschälte Zwiebel,
  grob zerschnitten
1 Teelöffel Salbei

2 Teelöffel Salz
1 Teelöffel Pfeffer
2 Liter Wasser
1/3 Tasse Karrotten, in Würfel
  geschnitten
1/3 Tasse Sellerie, in Würfel
  geschnitten
1/3 Tasse Zwiebel, in Würfel
  geschnitten

Die Erbsen mit soviel Wasser übergießen, daß etwa 5 cm Wasser über den Erbsen in einer Schüssel stehen. Über Nacht einweichen lassen. Den Schinkenknochen, das grob zerschnittene Gemüse, die Gewürz und die 2 Liter Wasser in einem großn Topf zum Kochen bringen. Dann bei schwacher Hitze 3 Stunden kochen lassen, gelegentlich umrühren. Die Brühe durch ein Sieb gießen und mit dem Schinkenknochen beiseite stellen. Die Erbsen abgießen. Die Erbsen und einen Liter Brühe in einen Topf geben und 3 Stunden lang bei schwacher Hitze kochen lassen. Dann die vom Knochen gelösten Schinkenstückchen und das in Würfel geschnittene Gemüse hinzugeben. Etwas mehr Brühe dazugießen, falls die Suppe zu dick ist. Eine Stunde bei schwacher Hitze kochen lassen.

BREAD SOUP (BROTSUPPE)

5 slices stale pumpernickel
  bread
1 cup water
3 to 4 cups apple juice
1 cup raisins

$^1/_4$ cup sugar
1 pound apples, peeled,
  chopped
1 piece lemon rind

Soak bread in water in saucepan for several hours. Bring to a boil, beating with wire whisk until smooth. Stir in apple juice, raisins, sugar, apples and lemon rind. Simmer over low heat until apples are tender but not mushy. Ladle into soup bowls. Garnish with fresh fruit and cinnamon if desired. May substitute dried fruit for apples. Yield: 4 servings.

BEET SALAD (ROTE RÜBENSALAT)

1 pound beets
$^1/_4$ cup vinegar
$^1/_4$ cup water
3 to 4 tablespoons olive oil
1 small onion, chopped

$^1/_2$ teaspoon sugar
2 teaspoons caraway seed
1 teaspoon cloves
1 bay leaf
Salt and pepper to taste

Cook beets in water to cover until tender; rinse with cold water. Peel beets and slice thinly. Combine remaining ingredients in bowl; mix well. Add beets. Marinate in refrigerator for several hours. Remove bay leaf before serving. Yield: 4 servings.

SAUERKRAUT SALAD (SAUERKRAUTSALAT)

1 16-ounce can sauerkraut
2 tart apples, peeled, grated
1 onion, chopped

3 tablespoons olive oil
1 teaspoon sugar
Salt and pepper to taste

Rinse sauerkraut under cold water; drain well. Combine remaining ingredients in serving dish. Add sauerkraut; toss to mix well. Let stand for 30 minutes before serving. Yield: 4 servings.

WINTER SALAD

1 cup chopped celery
6 ripe bananas, sliced
1 small head endive, chopped
1/4 cup oil
3 tablespoons vinegar

2 tablespoons white grape
  juice or wine
1/2 teaspoon salt
Pepper to taste

Blanch celery in boiling water in saucepan. Drain and cool celery. Combine with bananas and endive in salad bowl. Mix remaining ingredients in small bowl. Pour over salad; toss lightly to mix well. Yield: 8 servings.

WINTERSALAT

1 Tasse in Scheiben
  geschnittener Sellerie
6 reife, in Scheiben
  geschnittene Bananen
1 kleiner Kopf Endiviensalat,
  klein geschnitten

4 Eßlöffel Salatöl
3 Eßlöffel Essig
2 Eßlöffel Weißwein (nach
  Belieben)
1/2 Teelöffel Salz
Pfeffer nach Geschmack

Den Sellerie in kochendem Wasser in einem Top füberbrühen. Das Wasser abschütten, und den Sellerie erkalten lassen. Mit den Bananen und dem Endiviensalat in einer Salatschüssel vermischen. Die übrigen Zutaten in einer kleinen Schüssel vermischen. Über den Salat gießen und gut vermischen.

RADISH SALAD (RETTICHSALAT)

2 bunches radishes
Salt to taste
1 tablespoon olive oil
2 tablespoons vinegar

1 teaspoon chopped chives
Pepper to taste
1/2 cup sour cream, (optional)

Cut radishes into thin slices. Sprinkle with salt in bowl. Let stand for 10 minutes. Combine olive oil, vinegar, chives, salt and pepper in small bowl. Add to radishes. Marinate in refrigerator until serving time. Add sour cream at serving time. Yield: 4 servings.

BEEF ROULADEN

1¹/2 pounds round steak,
  ¹/4 inch thick
1 teaspoon salt
Pepper to taste
3 tablespoons finely chopped
  parsley
¹/4 cup chopped onion
3 strips lean bacon, cut into
  halves

¹/2 cup flour
2 tablespoons shortening
¹/2 cup bouillon
¹/2 cup water
2 tablespoons butter
2 tablespoons flour

Cut beef into 6 pieces. Pound thin with meat mallet. Sprinkle with salt, pepper, parsley and onion. Place 1 strip bacon on each piece of beef. Roll to enclose filling; secure with toothpick. Roll in ¹/2 cup flour, coating well. Brown in shortening in heavy saucepan. Add bouillon and water. Simmer, covered, for 2 hours. Remove beef rolls to serving platter; reserve ²/3 cup broth. Blend butter and 2 tablespoons flour in saucepan. Add reserved broth. Cook until thickened, stirring constantly. Serve with beef rolls. May bake beef in oven at 325° F. for 2¹/2 to 3 hours if preferred. Yield: 6 servings.

SAUERBRATEN

1   3 to 4-pound chuck roast
2 onions, thinly sliced
¹/2 lemon, thinly sliced
1¹/2 cups wine vinegar
2³/4 cups water
1 tablespoon sugar
6 cloves

2 bay leaves
¹/4 teaspoon ginger
1 tablespoon salt
2 tablespoons shortening
¹/4 cup water
¹/3 cup finely crushed
  gingersnaps

Combine roast, onions, lemon slices, vinegar, 2³/4 cups water, sugar and seasonings in large bowl. Marinate, covered, in refrigerator for 36 hours to 3 days. Turn roast several times; do not pierce with fork. Drain, reserving marinade. Pat roast dry with paper towels. Brown in shortening in heavy saucepan. Add reserved marinade. Simmer, covered, for 2 to 4 hours or until tender. Remove roast to serving platter. Strain cooking liquid; measure ³/4 cup. Combine with ¹/4 cup water and gingersnap crumbs in saucepan. Cook until thickened. Serve roast with gravy and noodles. Yield: 6 to 8 servings.

MEATBALLS WITH SPÄTZLE

1 pound ground beef	1 can beef broth
1/4 cup milk	1/2 cup chopped onion
1 egg, beaten	1 cup sour cream
1/4 cup dry bread crumbs	1 tablespoon flour
1 tablespoon chopped parsley	1/2 teaspoon caraway seed
1/4 teaspoon poultry seasoning	2 cups flour
Salt and pepper to taste	1 teaspoon salt
2 tablespoons oil	2 eggs, beaten
1 3-ounce can mushrooms, drained	1 cup milk

Combine ground beef with next 7 ingredients in bowl; mix well. Shape into 1 1/2-inch meatballs. Brown in oil in saucepan; drain. Add mushrooms, broth and onion. Simmer, covered, for 30 minutes. Stir in mixture of sour cream, 1 tablespoon flour and caraway seed. Cook until thickened, stirring constantly. Combine 2 cups flour with remaining ingredients in bowl; beat until mixture comes away from side of bowl. Place in colander. Press dough through colander with spoon into saucepan of boiling salted water. Cook for 5 minutes, stirring frequently; drain. Place in serving bowl. Spoon meatballs and sauce over top. Yield: 6 servings.

BIEROCKS

3 1/2 cups shredded cabbage	2 teaspoons sugar
2 tablespoons butter	1/4 cup warm water
1 pound ground beef	3/4 cup milk, scalded, cooled
Salt and pepper to taste	1/2 teaspoon shortening
1 package dry yeast	2 cups flour

Sauté cabbage in butter in skillet. Add ground beef. Cook until crumbly, stirring constantly; drain. Season to taste. Cool. Dissolve yeast and sugar in warm water in bowl; let stand for 5 minutes. Add milk, shortening and flour; mix well. Knead on floured surface until smooth and elastic. Place in greased bowl, turning to grease surface. Let rise, covered, for 30 minutes or until doubled in bulk. Roll into 1/4-inch thick rectangle on floured surface. Cut into eight 5-inch squares. Place 2 heaping tablespoons beef mixture on each square. Bring corners up to enclose filling; press edges to seal. Place seam side down on greased baking sheet. Let rise for 20 minutes. Bake at 375° F. for 30 minutes. Yield: 8 servings.

STUFFED CABBAGE ROLLS

1 head cabbage	1 large onion, sliced
1 pound ground beef	2 8-ounce cans tomato sauce
1/2 cup rice	2 29-ounce cans tomatoes
1 small onion, chopped	Juice of 2 lemons
2 eggs	1/2 cup packed brown sugar
Salt and pepper to taste	

Pour boiling water over cabbage in bowl. Let stand for several minutes to loosen leaves; drain. Combine ground beef, rice, chopped onion, eggs, salt and pepper in bowl. Remove 8 cabbage leaves. Spoon beef mixture into cabbage leaves. Roll to enclose filling. Line Dutch oven with additional cabbage leaves. Place cabbage rolls seam side down in Dutch oven. Top with sliced onion. Pour tomato sauce, tomatoes and lemon juice over top. Season to taste. Bring to a boil. Sprinkle with brown sugar. Bake, covered, at 375° F. for 1 hour. Bake, uncovered, for 2 hours. Yield: 8 servings.

PAPRIKA VEAL (PAPRIKA-RAHMSCHNITZEL)

1 pound veal cutlets	2 teaspoons flour
Salt to taste	1/2 cup cream
1/4 cup butter	Lemon slices
Paprika	Parsley

Pound veal with meat mallet. Season with salt to taste. Brown on both sides in butter in skillet. Sprinkle generously with paprika. Place on serving platter. Stir flour into pan drippings. Add cream. Cook until thickened, stirring constantly. Spoon over veal. Top with lemon slices and parsley. Yield: 4 servings.

FISH IN SOUR CREAM

3 pounds perch or pike	4 lemon slices
1/2 cup butter	1/4 cup bread crumbs
2 cups white wine	Salt and pepper to taste
3 anchovies, chopped	1 cup sour cream

Cut fish into serving pieces. Melt butter in saucepan. Stir in wine, anchovies, lemon slices, bread crumbs and seasonings. Add fish. Simmer for 20 minutes. Add sour cream. Heat just to the simmering point. Serve with boiled potatoes. Yield: 6 servings.

ROAST PORK (SCHWEINEBRATEN)

1 3½-pound pork loin	2 red apples, thinly sliced
Onion salt, marjoram, and	½ cup apple juice
pepper to taste	1 tablespoon brown sugar
4 cups drained sauerkraut	2 tablespoons butter

Sprinkle pork with onion salt, marjoram and pepper. Place in roasting pan. Place in 450° F. oven; reduce temperature to 350°. Roast for 1 hour and 45 minutes or to 185° F. on meat thermometer. Combine remaining ingredients in saucepan. Simmer for 5 to 10 minutes or just until apples are tender. Place roast on serving platter. Spoon apples around roast. Garnish with apple slices and parsley. Yield: 6 to 8 servings.

SCHNITZEL

6 pork loin cutlets, ½ inch	¾ cup dry bread crumbs
thick	1 teaspoon paprika
¼ cup flour	3 tablespoons shortening
1 teaspoon seasoned salt	¾ cup chicken broth
¼ teaspoon pepper	1 tablespoon flour
1 egg, beaten	¼ teaspoon dillweed
2 tablespoons milk	½ cup sour cream

Pound pork to ¼-inch thickness; slash edges. Coat with mixture of ¼ cup flour, seasoned salt and pepper. Combine egg and milk in bowl. Mix bread crumbs and paprika in bowl. Dip cutlets into egg mixture, then in crumbs. Brown in shortening in skillet for 3 minutes on each side. Remove to serving platter. Add broth to skillet, stirring to deglaze. Blend 1 tablespoon flour and dillweed with sour cream. Add to skillet. Cook until thickened, stirring constantly. Serve schnitzel with gravy and spätzle. Yield: 6 servings.

PEARS WITH BEANS AND BACON

3 cups water	Fresh savory to taste
Salt and white pepper to taste	1 pound small cooking pears
1 pound bacon	1 pound small potatoes, cooked
2 pounds green beans, broken	Cornstarch
into bite-sized pieces	Parsley

Bring water, salt and pepper to a boil in saucepan. Add bacon. Cook for 15 minutes. Add beans and savory. Cook for 15 minutes. Remove stems from pears. Place on beans. Simmer for 20 minutes. Drain mixture, reserving liquid. Place beans and bacon on serving platter. Place pears and potatoes around beans. Stir cornstarch into small amount of water. Add to reserved liquid in saucepan. Cook until thickened, stirring constantly. Pour over beans and pears. Garnish with parsley. Yield: 4 servings.

BIRNEN MIT BOHNEN UND SPECK

3/4 Liter Wasser	Frisches Bohnenkraut
Salz und weißer Pfeffer nach	1 Pfund kleine Kochbirnen
Geschmack	1 Pfund kleine Kartoffeln,
1 Pfund durchwachsener Speck	gekocht
2 Pfund grüne Bohnen, in	Stärkemehl
Stückchen gebrochen	Petersilie

Wasser, Salz und Pfeffer in einem Topf zum Kochen bringen. Speck hinzufügen. 15 Minuten lang kochen lassen. Bohnen und Bohnenkraut dazugeben. Weitere 15 Minuten kochen lassen. Birnen waschen und Stiele entfernen, dann auf die Bohnen legen. Bei niedriger Hitze 20 Minuten garen lassen. Die Flüssigkeit abgießen, aber aufbewahren. Bohnen und Speck auf einer Platte anrichten. Die Birnen und Kartoffeln um die Bohnen legen. Etwas Stärkemehl in einer kleinen Menge Wasser anrühren. Zu der aufbewahrten Flüssigkeit in einen Topf geben, unter ständigem Rühren erwärmen, bis die Flüssigkeit gedicht ist. Über die Bohnen und Birnen gießen. Mit Petersilie verzieren.

SWEET AND SOUR BEETS

2 cups tiny beets	1/2 teaspoon salt
1/3 cup sugar	1/3 cup vinegar
1 tablespoon flour	1 tablespoon butter
2 cloves	

Cook beets in boiling water to cover until tender. Drain and peel. Combine sugar, flour, cloves, salt and vinegar in double boiler; mix well. Cook until thickened and smooth, stirring constantly. Stir in butter and beets. Remove cloves. Heat to serving temperature. Yield: 4 servings.

BAVARIAN CABBAGE (BAYERISCHES KRAUT)

1 medium head red cabbage, shredded	2 juniper berries
	Salt and pepper to taste
1 tart apple, peeled, sliced	1/4 cup dry white wine
2 tablespoons butter	2 tablespoons cider vinegar
1 bay leaf	1 teaspoon sugar

Sauté cabbage and apple in butter in skillet for several minutes. Add bay leaf, juniper berries, salt and pepper. Simmer, covered, for 10 minutes. Add remaining ingredients, mix gently. Simmer for 30 minutes to 1 hour. Remove bay leaf. Yield: 4 to 6 servings.

HOT GERMAN POTATO AND BEAN SALAD

1 16-ounce can cut green beans	1 teaspoon salt
6 slices bacon	1/2 teaspoon caraway seed
1/2 cup chopped onion	1/3 cup vinegar
1 tablespoon sugar	3 cups cooked sliced potatoes
2 teaspoons flour	2 hard-boiled eggs, sliced

Drain beans, reserving 1/2 cup liquid. Brown bacon in skillet; drain on paper towel. Reserve 1/4 cup drippings. Sauté onion in reserved bacon drippings in skillet until tender-crisp but not brown. Stir in sugar, flour, salt and caraway seed. Add vinegar and reserved bean liquid. Cook until thickened, stirring constantly. Add beans and potatoes. Cook just until heated through, stirring gently. Spoon into serving dish. Crumble bacon over top. Garnish with hard-boiled eggs. Yield: 6 servings.

Photograph for this recipe on page 30.

POPPY SEED ROLLS (MOHNBRÖTCHEN)

1 package yeast
1 1/2 cups milk, scalded, cooled
   to lukewarm
1/2 teaspoon salt

4 cups flour
1 egg yolk, beaten
Poppy seed

Dissolve yeast in milk in mixer bowl. Let stand for several minutes. Stir in salt and just enough flour to make a thick batter. Let rise, covered, in warm place for several hours or until doubled in bulk. Add remaining flour; beat until mixture comes away from side of bowl. Knead on floured surface until smooth and elastic. Place in greased bowl, turning to grease surface. Let rise until doubled in bulk. Shape into rolls. Place on greased baking sheet. Let rise for 1 hour or until doubled in bulk. Brush with egg yolk; sprinkle with poppy seed. Bake at 375° F. for 20 minutes or until brown. Yield: 1 1/2 dozen.

POTATO TWISTS

1 1/2 packages yeast
1/2 cup lukewarm potato water
1 cup hot mashed potatoes
1 tablespoon melted shortening
2 tablespoons melted butter

1 teaspoon salt
1 1/2 tablespoons sugar
1 cup milk, scalded, cooled
6 cups (about) flour

Dissolve yeast in potato water. Combine mashed potatoes, shortening, butter, salt and sugar in large mixer bowl. Add milk; mix well. Add yeast mixture; mix well. Stir in enough flour gradually to form a dough which leaves side of bowl. Place in greased bowl, turning to grease surface. Let rise, covered, in warm place for 1 hour. Knead on floured surface until smooth and elastic, kneading in more flour if necessary to make a stiff dough. Place in greased bowl, turning to grease surface. Let rise until doubled in bulk. Knead again, chopping dough with knife for finer texture. Divide into 3 portions. Divide 1 portion into 3 parts. Roll each part into 10-inch rope. Braid ropes, pinching ends to seal. Repeat process with second portion. Place each in greased loaf pan. Divide remaining portion into 6 parts. Braid into 2 smaller braids. Moisten tops of larger braids with a small amount of milk. Place smaller braids on top. Brush with melted butter. Let rise until doubled in bulk. Bake at 450° F. until loaves begin to brown. Reduce temperature to 350°. Bake until loaves test done. Yield: 2 loaves.

APPLE CAKE

1 1/2 cups butter, softened
2 cups sugar
1/2 teaspoon vanilla extract
7 eggs

2 cups flour
1/4 teaspoon soda
6 large apples, peeled, sliced
Cinnamon-sugar

Cream butter and sugar in bowl until light. Add vanilla. Blend in eggs 1 at a time. Add flour and soda; mix well. Spread in greased 10 x 15-inch baking pan. Arrange apples over batter. Sprinkle with cinnamon-sugar. Bake at 350° F. for 40 minutes. Cool on wire rack. Yield: 12 servings.

BLACK FOREST CHERRY CAKE (SCHWARZWÄLDER TORTE)

1 package devil's food cake
   mix
1 small bottle of maraschino
   cherries

1 can cherry pie filling
1 cup whipping cream,
   whipped
Chocolate curls

Prepare and bake cake mix according to package directions for two 9-inch cake pans. Cool on wire rack. Drain cherries, reserving 2 tablespoons juice. Sprinkle over 1 cake layer. Spread with pie filling. Place remaining layer on top. Spread whipped cream over top and side of cake. Decorate with cherries and chocolate curls. Yield: 16 servings.

HAZELNUT TORTE (HASELNUSSE TORTE)

7 eggs, separated
3/4 cup confectioners' sugar
1/2 cup dry bread crumbs
1 cup finely ground hazelnuts
1 teaspoon lemon juice

Grated rind of 1/2 lemon
1/8 teaspoon cinnamon
1/4 teaspoon salt
Sweetened whipped cream

Beat egg yolks and confectioners' sugar in bowl until thick. Fold in next 5 ingredients. Beat egg whites and salt in bowl until stiff but not dry. Fold into egg yolk mixture. Spoon into 3 greased and waxed paper-lined 9-inch cake pans. Bake at 350° F. for 30 minutes. Cool on wire rack. Store, well covered, for 24 hours to ripen. Spread sweetened whipped cream between layers and on top of cake. Garnish with chopped hazelnuts. Yield: 12 servings.

APPLE STRUDEL (APFELSTRUDEL)

3/4 cup butter-flavored
   shortening
2 cups flour
1/2 teaspoon salt
2 egg yolks
1/2 cup water
5 apples, peeled, sliced

1 cup (scant) sugar
1 tablespoon flour
1 teaspoon cinnamon
1 cup (scant) confectioners'
   sugar
2 tablespoons milk
1 teaspoon vanilla extract

Cut shortening into mixture of 2 cups flour and salt in bowl. Add egg yolks and water; mix to form a sticky dough. Chill in refrigerator. Divide into 2 portions. Roll 1 portion very thin on floured surface. Place on lightly oiled baking sheet. Arrange apple slices in rows on pastry. Sprinkle with mixture of sugar, 1 tablespoon flour and cinnamon. Roll remaining pastry very thin. Place over apples. Turn up edges of bottom pastry; seal and flute edges. Bake at 375° F. for 45 minutes. Mix remaining ingredients in bowl. Spread over warm strudel. Cut into squares. Yield: 24 servings.

BERLIN WREATHS (BERLINER KRÄNZE)

3/4 cup shortening
3/4 cup butter, softened
1 cup sugar
2 teaspoons grated orange rind
2 eggs

4 cups sifted flour
1 egg white
2 tablespoons sugar
Candied green citron
Candied red cherries, chopped

Cream shortening, butter and 1 cup sugar in mixer bowl until light and fluffy. Add orange rind and eggs; mix well. Mix in flour. Chill dough in refrigerator. Roll small amounts into 1/4 x 6-inch ropes. Shape ropes into wreathes, looping ends and leaving 1/2-inch ends free. Place on cookie sheet. Beat egg white in bowl until soft peaks form. Add 2 tablespoons sugar gradually, beating until stiff peaks form. Spread evenly on cookies. Add leaves cut from green citron and place cherries in center of knot. Bake at 400° F. for 10 to 12 minutes or until set but not brown. Cool on wire rack. Yield: 6 dozen.

MANDARIN ORANGE DESSERT

1 envelope unflavored gelatin
1/4 cup water
Juice of 4 mandarin oranges
1 cup eggnog or egg liqueur
    (Advocat)

1/4 cup sugar
1 vanilla bean
1/2 cup whipping cream

Soften gelatin in water in saucepan. Combine orange juice, eggnog and sugar in mixer bowl. Split vanilla bean lengthwise and scrape out pulp. Add to orange juice mixture. Beat until foamy. Heat gelatin until completely dissolved, stirring constantly. Add gradually to orange juice mixture, beating constantly. Chill until partially set. Beat cream in bowl until soft peaks form. Fold gently into partially congealed mixture. Spoon into dessert glasses. Chill until set. Garnish with orange slices. Yield: 4 servings.

MANDARINENDESSERT

1 Päckchen weiße Gelatine
4 Eßlöffel Wasser
Saft von 4 Mandarinen
1/4 Liter Eierlikör

4 Eßlöffel Zucker
1 Vanilleschotte
1/8 Liter Sahne

Die Gelatine in das Wasser in einen Topf geben. Mandarinensaft, Likör und Zucker in einer Schüssel vermischen. Die Vanilleschote der Länge nach spalten und die Samen daraus kratzen. Zu dem Mardarinensaftgemisch geben. Rühren, bis es schaumig wird. Die Gelatine erwärmen, ständig rühren, bis sie ganz aufgelöst ist. Unter ständigem Rühren langsam in das Mandarinensaftgemisch geben. Kalt stellen, bis es anfängt zu gelieren. Die Sahne in einer Schüssel schlagen, bis sie steif wird. Vorsichtig unter die halb gelierte Masse ziehen. In Dessertschälchen geben. Kalt stellen. Mit Orangenscheiben verzieren.

BEE STINGS

1 package yeast	6 to 7 cups flour
1 teaspoon sugar	1/2 cup butter
2 cups lukewarm milk	3/4 cup sugar
10 tablespoons sugar	2 tablespoons milk
1/4 cup butter, softened	1 tablespoon honey
1/4 cup shortening	1/3 cup (or more) sliced
1 egg	almonds
Salt to taste	

Dissolve yeast and 1 teaspoon sugar in 2 cups lukewarm milk in bowl. Add 10 tablespoons sugar, 1/4 cup butter, shortening, egg and salt; mix well. Mix in flour until dough pulls away from side of bowl. Knead on floured surface until smooth and elastic. Place in greased bowl, turning to grease surface. Let rise, covered, in warm place until doubled in bulk. Bring 1/2 cup butter, 3/4 cup sugar, 2 tablespoons milk, honey and almonds to a boil in saucepan. Cool slightly. Grease 10 x 15-inch baking pan. Attach greased collar of aluminum foil to extend sides. Punch dough down. Pat into prepared pan. Pour almond mixture over top. Let rise until doubled in bulk. Bake at 375° F. for 30 to 40 minutes or until golden. Cool. Cut into strips. Slice strips into 2 layers. Spread bottom layers with Vanilla Buttercream. Replace tops. Cut into desired lengths.

Vanilla Buttercream

1 cup butter, softened	1 to 2 teaspoons vanilla extract
1 or 2 egg yolks	3/4 cup confectioners' sugar

Cream butter in mixer bowl until light and fluffy. Blend in egg yolks and vanilla. Add confectioners' sugar gradually, beating until smooth.

BIENENSTICH

1 Päckchen Hefe	Salz nach Geschmack
1 Teelöffel Zucker	750-875 Gramm Mehl
1/2 Liter lauwarme Milch	125 Gramm Butter
10 Eßlöffel Zucker	175 Gramm Zucker
4 Eßlöffel Butter, weich	2 Eßlöffel Milch
geworden	1 Eßlöffel Honig
4 Eßlöffel Backfett	50 Gramm (oder mehr) in
1 Ei	Scheiben geschnittene Mandeln

Die Hefe und 1 Teelöffel Zucker in der lauwarmen Milch auflösen, gut vermischen. Das Mehl darunter mischen, bis der Teig sich von der Seite der Schüssel löst. Auf einer mit Mehl bestäubten Fläche kneten, bis der Teig weich und elastisch ist. In eine gefettete Schüssel geben. Zudecken, an einem warmen Platz gehen lassen, bis er doppelt so groß ist. 125 Gramm Butter, 175 Gramm Zucker, 2 Eßlöffel Milch, Honig und Mandeln in einem Topf zum Kochen bringen. Abkühlen lassen. Ein 25 x 37 cm großes Backblech einfetten. Einen eingefetteten Kragen aus Alufolie an den Seiten anbringen. Den aufgegangenen Teig mit der Hand zusammendrucken, auf das vorbereitete Blech ausrollen und die Seiten hochstellen. Das Mandelgemisch gleichmäßig darüber geben. Aufgehen lassen, bis der Teig zweimal so hoch ist. Bei 375 Grad 30 bis 40 Minuten backen, bis der Belag goldgelb ist. Abkühlen. In Streifen schneiden. Diese in der Waagerechten durchschneiden. Die untere Schicht mit Vanillebuttercreme bestreichen. Die obere Schicht darüber legen. In die gewünschte Länge schneiden.

Vanillebuttercreme

250 Gramm Butter, weich
1 oder 2 Eigelb

1 bis 2 Teelöffel Vanilleextrakt
100 Gramm Puderzucker

Die Butter in eine Schüssel schaumig rühren. Eigelb und Vanilleextrakt darunter geben. Puderzucker langsam dazugeben und alles zu einer lockeren glatten Creme aufschlagen.

BREAD PUDDING (BROTPUDDING)

6 tablespoons sugar
3 cups milk
10 slices white bread
10 slices brown bread
2 tablespoons melted butter
1 tablespoon flour

1/4 cup raisins
3 tablespoons candied lemon
 peel
1 cup chopped almonds
Confectioners' sugar

Combine sugar and milk in bowl, stirring until sugar is dissolved. Crumble bread into milk. Let stand for 1 hour. Add butter, flour, raisins, lemon peel and almonds; mix well. Spoon into pudding mold; cover tightly. Steam for 20 minutes. Invert onto serving plate. Sprinkle with confectioners' sugar.
Yield: 6 servings.

CUCINA ITALIANA

ITALY

SPAGHETTI WITH MEAT SAUCE

1 pound beef, finely chopped
1/4 cup olive oil
1 onion, chopped
1 cup chopped mushrooms
1 clove of garlic, chopped
1 tablespoon chopped parsley

1 large can tomatoes
1/2 teaspoon oregano
1 bay leaf
Salt and pepper to taste
1 pound spaghetti

Brown beef in olive oil in saucepan. Add onion, mushrooms, garlic and parsley. Cook for 10 minutes, stirring constantly. Add tomatoes and seasonings. Simmer until of desired consistency. Remove bay leaf. Cook spaghetti *al dente* in boiling water in saucepan; drain. Place spaghetti on serving platter. Top with meat sauce. Garnish with cheese. Yield: 4 servings.

SPAGHETTI AL RAGÙ

1 libbra di manzo tritato
  finemente
1/4 di tazza di olio di oliva
1 cipolla tritata
1 tazza di funghi tritati
1 spicchio di aglio tritato

1 grossa scatola di pomodori
1/2 cucchiaino di origano
1 foglia di alloro
Sale e pepe a piacere
1 libbra di spaghetti

Rosolare la carne nell'olio in una padella. Aggiungere cipolla, funghi, aglio e prezzemolo. Cuocere per 10 minuti, senza smettere di mescolare. Aggiungere pomodori e condimenti. Cuocere a fuoco basso fino a raggiungere la consistenza adatta. Eliminare la foglia di alloro. Cuocere gli spaghetti al dente in acqua salata in ebollizione; scolarli. Sistemare gli spaghetti in un piatto di portata. Condirli con il ragù ed il formaggio.

ANTIPASTO

8 ounces tiny onions
1 head cauliflower, broken
  into flowerets
2 green peppers, chopped
1 pound small mushrooms
1 cup sliced carrots
1 cup sliced celery
1 1/2 cups olive oil

2 cups dry white wine
1 cup vinegar
2 cloves of garlic, minced
1 bay leaf
1 10-ounce can tomato purée
Salt and pepper
2 6-ounce cans tuna
1/2 cup sliced dill pickles

Sauté onions, cauliflower, green peppers, mushrooms, carrots and celery in olive oil in skillet. Reduce heat. Simmer, covered, for 5 minutes, stirring occasionally. Add wine, vinegar, garlic and bay leaf. Simmer until liquid is reduced by 1/3. Stir in tomato purée. Simmer, covered, for 10 minutes. Add salt and pepper to taste. Remove bay leaf. Add tuna and pickles; mix gently. Pour into bowl. Chill in refrigerator. Spoon onto platter or individual plates. Garnish with anchovies. Yield: 20 servings.

MARINATED ARTICHOKE HEARTS
(CARCINOFINI PER ANTIPASTO)

1 10-ounce package frozen
  artichoke hearts
1/2 cup olive oil

2 tablespoons lemon juice
1/4 teaspoon oregano
Salt and pepper to taste

Cook artichoke hearts according to package directions; drain and cool. Combine remaining ingredients in bowl; mix well. Add artichokes. Marinate in refrigerator for 3 hours or longer. Yield: 4 servings.

CHICK-PEA APPETIZER (CECI)

1 16-ounce can chick-peas
1 tablespoon olive oil
1/2 cup chopped pine nuts

3 tablespoons minced parsley
Salt and pepper to taste
1 small can anchovy fillets

Bring undrained chick peas to a boil in saucepan; drain, Press through a sieve into bowl. Add olive oil, pine nuts, parsley and seasonings; mix well. Shape into balls. Wrap anchovy fillet around each ball; secure with toothpick. Place on buttered baking sheet. Bake at 400° F. for 15 to 20 minutes or until light brown. Serve at once. Yield: 6 to 8 servings.

MINESTRONE

1 cup dried white beans
1 onion, chopped
1 clove of garlic, minced
1 leek, chopped
1/4 cup chopped parsley
1 teaspoon thyme
1/2 cup olive oil
1 tablespoon tomato paste
1/4 cup water

1 16-ounce can tomatoes
3 stalks celery, chopped
2 carrots, chopped
2 potatoes, chopped
2 cups shredded cabbage
2 zucchini, chopped
6 cups bouillon
Salt and pepper to taste
4 ounces spaghetti, broken

Soak beans in water to cover in saucepan overnight. Drain beans. Add fresh water to cover. Simmer until beans are tender; drain. Sauté onion, garlic, leek, parsley and thyme in olive oil in large saucepan. Add mixture of tomato paste and 1/4 cup water. Simmer for 5 minutes. Add remaining ingredients except spaghetti. Simmer, covered, for 1 hour. Stir in beans and spaghetti. Cook just until spaghetti is tender. Serve with Parmesan cheese. Yield: 6 to 8 servings.

SPINACH SOUP (ZUPPA DI SPINACI)

2 pounds fresh spinach,
    chopped
8 cups chicken broth
1/2 teaspoon nutmeg
1 teaspoon salt

1/4 teaspoon pepper
1/4 cup olive oil
4 eggs
1/3 cup Parmesan cheese

Cook spinach in 1 cup boiling broth in saucepan for 5 minutes. Drain, reserving broth. Combine reserved broth with remaining broth in saucepan. Bring to a boil. Sauté spinach with nutmeg, salt and pepper in olive oil in saucepan for 2 minutes. Beat eggs with cheese in bowl. Add to spinach; mix well. Add boiling broth very gradually, stirring constantly. Simmer for 2 minutes or until thickened. Yield: 6 to 8 servings.

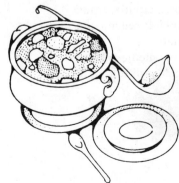

PASTA AND BEAN SOUP

1 pound dried pinto beans
3 tablespoons olive oil
2 tablespoons flour
8 cups warm water
1 clove of garlic, crushed
1 large onion, chopped
4 stalks celery with leaves,
   chopped
2 medium carrots, chopped

2 tablespoons olive oil
1/2 cup butter
1 28-ounce can tomatoes
1/2 cup packed chopped parsley
2 10-ounce cans beef broth
1 tablespoon basil
Salt and pepper to taste
8 ounces shell macaroni

Soak beans in water to cover in bowl overnight. Rinse and drain beans. Combine with 3 tablespoons olive oil and flour in large saucepan; shake to coat well. Add warm water and garlic. Simmer, covered, for 1 1/4 hours. Sauté onion, celery and carrots in 2 tablespoons olive oil and butter in large skillet for 5 minutes. Add tomatoes and parsley. Simmer, covered, for 1 hour, adding water if necessary to prevent sticking. Reserve 3 cups bean mixture. Process remaining beans and sautéed vegetables in food processor. Combine with beef broth, reserved beans, basil, salt and pepper in saucepan. Simmer for 15 minutes, adding water if necessary for desired consistency. Cook macaroni in salted boiling water in saucepan until tender; drain. Stir macaroni into soup. Yield: 6 to 8 servings.

Photograph for this recipe on page 48.

MINESTRA CON PASTA E FAGIOLI

1 libbra di fagioli borlotti
   secchi
3 cucchiai di olio di oliva
2 cucchiai di farina
8 tazze di acqua calda
1 spicchio di aglio schiacciato
1 grossa cipolla, tritata
4 gambi di sedano con fogli
   tritati
2 carote medie tritate
2 cucchiai di olio di oliva

1/2 tazza di burro
1 scatole di pomodori da
   28 once
1/2 tazza ben colma di
   prezzemolo tritato
2 scatole di brodo di carne da
   10 once
1 cucchiaio di basilico
Sale e pepe a piacere
8 once di pasta a conchiglie

Mettere a bagno i fagioli ricoperti d'acqua per un'intera notte. Risciacquare e scolare i fagioli. Mettere i fagioli in una pentola capace e unirvi 3 cucchiai di olio di oliva e la farina; scuotere per distribuire il condimento. Aggiungere l'acqua calda e l'aglio. Incoperchiare e cuocere a fuoco basso per 1 ora e 1/4. Rosolare cipolla, sedano e carote in 2 cuccchiai di olio di oliva e burro in una padella capace per 5 minuti. Aggiungere pomodori e prezzemolo. Cuocere a fuoco basso, incoperchiati, per 1 ora, aggiungendo dell'acqua se fosse necessario per evitare che attacchi al fondo. Tenere da parte 3 tazze della miscela di fagioli. Tritare nel frullatore il resto dei fagioli e delle verdure rosolate. Mettere in una pentola insieme al brodo di carne, ai fagioli messi da parte, al basilico e condire con sale e pepe. Cuocere per 15 minuti, aggiungendo dell'acqua per ottenere la consistenza adatta. Cuocere la pasta in acqua bollente salata; scolarla. Aggiungere la pasta alla minestra.

BAKED LASAGNA (LASAGNE AL FORNO)

1 pound ground beef
1 clove of garlic, minced
1 8-ounce can tomato sauce
2 1/2 cups chopped tomatoes
1/2 teaspoon oregano
1 teaspoon salt
1/4 teaspoon pepper

8 ounces wide lasagna noodles
1 pound cottage or ricotta
 cheese
1/2 cup Parmesan cheese
2 cups shredded mozzarella
 cheese

Brown ground beef with garlic in saucepan, stirring until beef is crumbly; drain. Add tomato sauce, tomatoes and seasonings. Simmer for 30 minutes. Cook noodles in boiling salted water in saucepan just until tender; drain. Spread 1 1/2 cups meat sauce in greased 9 x 13-inch baking dish. Layer half the noodles, half the cottage cheese, half the Parmesan cheese and 1/3 of the mozzarella cheese over meat sauce. Repeat layers. Top with remaining meat sauce and mozzarella cheese. Bake at 350° F. for 45 minutes. Let stand for 15 minutes.
Yield: 8 servings.

MARZETTI

1 1/2 pounds ground chuck
2 medium onions, chopped
2 medium green peppers,
  chopped
1 cup chopped celery
1 8-ounce can sliced
  mushrooms, drained

3 cups curly egg noodles
4 cups tomato juice
1/4 teaspoon garlic powder
2 tablespoons chili powder
1 teaspoon salt
1/4 teaspoon pepper
1/4 cup Parmesan cheese

Brown ground chuck in saucepan, stirring until crumbly; drain. Add remaining ingredients except cheese; mix well. Simmer, covered, for 35 minutes. Spoon into serving bowl. Sprinkle with cheese. Let stand for 5 minutes. Serve hot or cold. Yield: 8 servings.

RAVIOLI WITH MEAT SAUCE
(RAVIOLI CON SALSA DI CARNE)

1 pound ground beef
2 onions, chopped
2 tablespoons oil
1 cup tomato paste
1 cup water
1 20-ounce can tomatoes
1 clove of garlic, minced
1 tablespoon sugar
1/2 cup ricotta cheese

1 10-ounce package frozen
  chopped spinach, cooked
3 ounces cream cheese,
  softened
1/4 cup Italian bread crumbs
Salt and pepper to taste
2 cups flour
3 eggs, beaten

Brown ground beef and onions in oil in skillet, stirring until ground beef is crumbly; drain. Add mixture of tomato paste and water, tomatoes, garlic and sugar; mix well. Simmer for 30 minutes. Combine ricotta cheese, spinach, cream cheese, bread crumbs, salt and pepper in bowl; set aside. Mix flour and eggs in bowl. Add enough water to bind. Roll very thin on floured surface. Cut into 1 1/4-inch squares. Place a small amount of spinach mixture in center of each square. Fold over to enclose filling, forming triangle. Seal edges. Drop into boiling salted water in saucepan. Simmer until tender; drain. Place in serving dish. Pour meat sauce over top. Serve with Parmesan cheese.

VEAL PARMIGIANA (VITELLO ALLA PARMIGIANA)

¹/3 cup Parmesan cheese
1 teaspoon oregano
1¹/2 pounds veal cutlets

¹/2 teaspoon salt
¹/4 teaspoon pepper
¹/4 cup olive oil

Mix Parmesan cheese and crumbled oregano in shallow dish. Pound veal ¹/4 inch thick with meat mallet. Sprinkle with salt and pepper. Roll in cheese mixture, coating well. Sauté in hot olive oil in skillet for 4 minutes on each or until golden brown. Yield: 4 to 6 servings.

VEAL PICCATA

1¹/2 to 2 pounds thinly sliced
  veal
¹/4 cup flour
6 tablespoons butter
¹/2 teaspoon salt

¹/4 teaspoon freshly ground
  pepper
Juice of 1¹/2 lemons
10 sprigs of parsley, chopped

Pound veal very thin with meat mallet. Dip slices in flour; shake off excess. Brown on both sides in butter in skillet. Sprinkle with salt and pepper. Reduce heat. Cook for 5 minutes. Add lemon juice and parsley. Cook for 1 minute longer. Place veal on serving plate. Spoon pan juices over top. Yield: 4 to 6 servings.

PICCATA DI VITELLO

1¹/2 - 2 libbre di vitello a
  fettine sottili
¹/4 di tazza di farina
6 cucchiai di burro
¹/2 cucchiaino di sale

¹/4 di cucchiaino di pepe
  macinato
Succo di 1 limone e ¹/2
10 rametti di prezzemolo da
  tritare

Battere le fettine di vitello per renderle molto sottili. Infarinare le fettine; scuoterle per eliminare l'eccesso di farina. Rosolarle nel burro in padella, lasciandole dorare dalle due parti. Condire con sale e pepe. Ridurre il calore, cuocere per 5 minuti. Aggiungere il succo di limone ed il prezzemolo. Cuocere per un altro minuto. Sistemare il vitello sul piatto di portata. Ricoprirlo con il sugo di cottura.

CHICKEN CACCIATORE

1 4-pound chicken, cut up	1 carrot, sliced
1 clove of garlic, crushed	1/2 cup chicken stock
1/3 cup olive oil	1/2 teaspoon oregano
1 pound tomatoes, peeled,	1 teaspoon salt
chopped	1/4 teaspoon pepper
1 large onion, sliced	4 ounces fresh mushrooms,
1 large green pepper, chopped	sliced
1 stalk celery, chopped	

Sauté chicken and garlic in olive oil in heavy saucepan for 10 minutes. Add tomatoes, onion, green pepper, celery, carrot, stock and seasonings; mix well. Simmer, covered, for 40 minutes, stirring occasionally. Add water if necessary for desired consistency. Stir in mushrooms. Cook for 15 minutes longer. Serve with pasta or polenta. Yield: 5 servings.

POLLA ALLA CACCIATORA

4 libbre di pollo a pezzi	1 carota affettata
1 spicchio di aglio schiacciato	1/2 tazza di brodo di pollo
1/3 di tazza di olio de oliva	1/2 cucchiaino di origano
1 libbra di pomodori pelati	1 cucchiaino di sale
tritati	1/4 di cucchiaino di pepe
1 grossa cipolla affettata	4 once di funghi freschi
1 grosso peperone verde tritato	affettati
1 gambo di sedano tritato	

Rosolare il pollo con l'aglio nell'olio di oliva in una pentola pesante per 10 minuti. Aggiungere pomodori, cipolla, peperone verde, sedano, carota, brodo e condimenti; rimestare con cura. Incoperchiare e cuocere a fuoco basso per 40 minuti, rimestando ogni tanto. Aggiungere acqua se fosse necessario per raggiungere la consistenza adatta. Aggiungere i funghi. Cuocere per altri 15 minuti. Servire con pasta o polenta.

ZESTY CHICKEN ITALIANO

1 pound chicken breast filets
2 tablespoons butter
1 clove of garlic, minced
1¹/2 cups thinly sliced zucchini
1¹/2 cups sliced fresh
   mushrooms
1 15-ounce can tomato sauce

1 16-ounce can tomatoes
1¹/2 teaspoons oregano
¹/2 teaspoon lemon pepper
¹/8 teaspoon cayenne pepper
8 ounces vermicelli
Parmesan cheese

Cut chicken into 1-inch pieces. Sauté in butter in saucepan. Add garlic, zucchini and mushrooms. Sauté for 2 minutes. Stir in tomato sauce, tomatoes and seasonings. Simmer for 10 minutes or until sauce is of desired consistency. Cook vermicelli according to package directions; drain. Place on serving platter. Spoon chicken and sauce over top. Sprinkle with cheese. Yield: 4 servings.

Photograph for this recipe on Cover.

PIZZA

1 package dry yeast
¹/4 cup lukewarm water
2 teaspoons sugar
1 teaspoon salt
1 tablespoon shortening
³/4 cup water
4 cups flour
2 tablespoons oil

2 8-ounce cans Italian-style
   tomato sauce
2 cups shredded mozzarella
   cheese
8 ounces sliced pepperoni
1 cup sliced mushrooms
1 cup sliced olives
Oregano and pepper to taste

Dissolve yeast in ¹/4 cup lukewarm water. Combine sugar, salt, shortening, ³/4 cup water and 1 cup flour in mixer bowl; beat until smooth. Add yeast mixture; mix well. Stir in enough remaining flour to make a stiff dough. Knead on floured surface until smooth and elastic. Place in greased bowl, turning to grease surface. Let rise, covered, in warm place for 1 hour or until doubled in bulk. Divide dough into 2 portions. Roll each portion into thin circle on floured surface. Fit into 2 greased pizza pans. Brush with oil. Spread with tomato sauce. Sprinkle with mozzarella cheese, pepperoni, mushrooms, olives and seasonings. Bake at 450° F. for 20 minutes. Yield: 6 to 8 servings.

SICILIAN-STYLE FISH (PESCE ALLA SICILIANA)

2 pounds halibut or swordfish,
  cut into thick steaks
1/4 cup olive oil
1 tablespoon chopped parsley
1 clove of garlic, minced
1/2 cup white vinegar

2 pounds tomatoes, peeled,
  chopped
Salt and pepper to taste
1 10-ounce package frozen
  peas

Brown fish in hot olive oil in skillet. Add parsley, garlic and vinegar. Cook until liquid has almost evaporated. Add tomatoes and seasonings. Simmer, covered, for 5 minutes. Stir in peas. Simmer, covered, for 30 minutes. Place fish on serving platter. Pour sauce over top. Yield: 4 to 6 servings.

SHRIMP MARINARA (SCAMPI ALLA MARINARA)

6 tablespoons butter
1/4 cup olive oil
2 ounces salt pork, minced
2 onions, chopped
28 jumbo shrimp, peeled
1/2 cup flour
3 cloves of garlic, crushed
1/4 cup chopped fresh parsley
1 tablespoon oregano

1/2 teaspoon salt
1/4 teaspoon pepper
Red pepper to taste
4 tomatoes, chopped
2 tablespoons tomato paste
2 bay leaves
1/2 cup dry white wine
1/4 cup warm water

Heat butter, olive oil and salt pork in large skillet until butter is melted. Add onions. Sauté until medium brown. Roll shrimp in flour, coating well. Add to skillet. Sauté for 5 minutes. Stir in garlic, parsley, oregano, salt, pepper and red pepper. Cook for 5 minutes, stirring constantly. Add remaining ingredients. Simmer, covered, for 20 minutes. Simmer, uncovered, for 5 minutes longer. Remove bay leaves. Serve on rice or pasta. Garnish with Parmesan cheese.
Yield: 4 to 6 servings.

EGGPLANT PARMIGIANA

1 large eggplant
Salt and pepper to taste
1 cup fine dry bread crumbs
2 eggs, lightly beaten
Oil for frying

1 1/2 cups tomato sauce, heated
8 ounces mozzarella cheese,
  sliced
1 teaspoon basil
1/4 cup Parmesan cheese

Cut unpeeled eggplant into 1/4-inch slices. Sprinkle with salt and pepper. Coat slices with bread crumbs; dip in eggs then in bread crumbs again. Chill for 30 minutes. Heat 1/8 inch oil in skillet. Fry eggplant until golden brown on both sides, adding oil if necessary. Drain on paper towels. Alternate layers of tomato sauce, eggplant, mozzarella cheese, tomato sauce, basil and Parmesan cheese in shallow 2-quart baking dish until all ingredients are used. Bake at 350° F. for 25 to 30 minutes. Yield: 6 servings.

PARMIGIANA DI MELANZANE

1 grossa melanzana
Sale e pepe
1 tazza di pane grattuggiato
  fine
2 uova leggermente sbattute
Olio per friggere

1 tazza e 1/2 di salsa di
  pomodoro calda
8 once di mozzarella affettata
1 cucchiaino di basilico
1/4 di tazza di Parmigiano

Tagliare la melanzana a fette (spessore 1/4 di pollice), senza pelarla. Spolverizzare con il sale e pepe. Passare le fette nel pane grattuggiato; metterle nell'uovo e poi passarle di nuovo nel pane grattuggiato. Metterle in frigorifero per 30 minuti. Scaldare circa 1/8 di pollice di olio in una padella. Friggere la melanzana lasciandola dorare dalle due parti, aggiungendo dell'olio se fosse necessario. Sgocciolarle ed appoggiarle su una carta assorbente. Alternare strati di salsa di pomodoro, fette di melanzana, fettine di mozzarella, salsa di pomodoro, basilico e Parmigiano in una teglia poco profonda, con una capacità di 2 quarti, fino all'esaurimento degli ingredienti. Cuocere in forno a 350° F. per 25-30 minuti.

MUSHROOMS WITH PINE NUTS (FUNGHI CON PINOLI)

1 pound fresh mushrooms,
  sliced
3 tablespoons butter
1/2 cup finely chopped onion

1/2 cup pine nuts
3 tablespoons dry white wine
Salt and pepper to taste

Sauté mushrooms in butter in skillet for 3 minutes. Add remaining ingredients. Cook for 4 to 5 minutes longer or until vegetables are tender and pine nuts are golden. Yield: 4 servings.

FRIED PEPPERS (PEPERONI FRITTI)

8 large sweet peppers (green,
  red and yellow)
1 clove of garlic, minced

1/3 cup olive oil
1/2 teaspoon salt
1/4 teaspoon pepper

Slice peppers lengthwise into 1-inch wide strips. Sauté garlic in olive oil in skillet for 1 minute. Add peppers, salt and pepper. Cook over medium heat for 5 minutes, stirring constantly. Reduce heat. Simmer, covered, for 15 minutes or just until peppers are tender. Serve hot or cold as vegetable, antipasto or accompaniment for meats, rice, polenta or eggs. Yield: 6 to 8 servings.

RED AND GREEN VEGETABLES (LEGUMI ROSSI E VERDI)

3 onions, sliced
2 tablespoons oil
2 green peppers, cut into strips
2 cups chopped tomatoes

1/2 cabbage, cut into small
  wedges
Salt and pepper to taste
1 tablespoon oregano

Sauté onions in oil in skillet. Add green peppers. Cook covered, for 5 minutes. Stir in tomatoes, cabbage and seasonings. Simmer, covered, for 15 minutes or until vegetables are tender; add a small amount of water if necessary to prevent sticking. Yield: 4 servings.

STUFFED ZUCCHINI (ZUCCHINI RIPIENA)

2 medium zucchini
1 medium onion, chopped
2 tablespoons olive oil
1/2 cup chopped peeled tomato
2 tablespoons capers
1/4 cup chopped black olives

1/4 teaspoon oregano
1/4 teaspoon basil
Salt and pepper to taste
1/4 cup dry bread crumbs
1/4 cup Parmesan cheese
2 tablespoons olive oil

Cut zucchini into halves lengthwise. Remove pulp, reserving 1/4-inch shells. Chop pulp. Sauté onion in 2 tablespoons olive oil in skillet. Stir in chopped zucchini. Sauté for 5 minutes. Add tomato, capers, olives and seasonings. Cook over medium heat for 10 minutes, stirring occasionally. Stir in bread crumbs and half the cheese. Spoon into reserved shells. Top with remaining cheese. Drizzle with 2 tablespoons olive oil. Bake, covered, at 375° F. for 40 minutes. Bake, uncovered, for 10 minutes longer. Yield: 4 servings.

BROCCOLI FRITTATA

1 bunch broccoli, chopped
4 eggs
1 clove of garlic, minced

3 tablespoons Parmesan cheese
Salt and pepper to taste
2 tablespoons olive oil

Cook broccoli in water in saucepan until tender-crisp; drain. Beat eggs with garlic, cheese and seasonings in bowl. Stir in broccoli. Heat olive oil in skillet. Add egg mixture. Cook over low heat for 5 minutes or until lightly browned. Turn with spatula. Cook until light brown. Serve immediately. Yield: 4 servings.

RICE AND PEAS (RISI E BISI)

1 onion, finely chopped
1/4 cup finely chopped ham or
   prosciutto
1/2 cup butter
1 1/2 cups long grain rice

3 cups shelled fresh peas
3 1/2 cups hot chicken broth
1 teaspoon salt
1/4 teaspoon pepper
1/4 cup Parmesan cheese

Sauté onion and ham in butter in saucepan over medium heat for 5 minutes. Add rice. Sauté for 5 minutes or until rice is translucent. Stir in peas, broth and seasonings. Simmer, covered, for 20 minutes, stirring occasionally. Stir in cheese. Serve with additional cheese. Yield: 6 to 8 servings.

FETTUCINI

6 ounces fettucini
1/2 cup butter, softened
1/4 cup heavy cream

1 tablespoon fresh parsley
1/2 cup Parmesan cheese

Cook noodles according to package directions; drain. Heat baking dish at 250° F. for 10 minutes. Beat butter and cream in mixer bowl until smooth. Add parsley and cheese. Place pasta in heated baking dish. Pour cream sauce over top. Bake for 2 to 5 minutes longer. Toss gently. Serve immediately. Yield: 4 servings.

SPINACH NOODLES WITH GREEN SAUCE
(PASTA AL PESTO)

2 cloves of garlic
1 tablespoon pine nuts
1 cup packed basil leaves
1 bunch parsley, stems
   removed

Salt to taste
6 tablespoons Parmesan cheese
1/3 cup oil
8 ounces spinach noodles

Combine garlic, pine nuts, basil, parsley, salt and cheese in blender container. Process until smooth. Add oil gradually, processing to form a thick, creamy sauce. Cook noodles *al dente* in boiling water in saucepan; drain. Place in serving dish. Pour sauce over top. Serve with additional Parmesan cheese.
Yield: 4 servings.

SPAGHETTI WITH FOUR CHEESES
(SPAGHETTI AL QUATTRO FORMAGGI)

16 ounces spaghetti
2/3 cup shredded mozzarella
   cheese
2/3 cup shredded Gouda cheese

2/3 cup shredded Swiss cheese
Salt and pepper to taste
1/2 cup melted butter
2/3 cup Parmesan cheese

Cook spaghetti *al dente* in salted boiling water in saucepan; drain. Place in heated serving dish. Add mozzarella and Gouda cheeses; toss to mix well. Add Swiss cheese, salt, pepper and 1/4 cup butter; toss to mix well. Add remaining 1/4 cup butter and Parmesan cheese; toss lightly. Serve immediately.
Yield: 4 servings.

BREAD STICKS (GRISSINI)

1 package dry yeast	1 teaspoon salt
2/3 cup warm water	2 cups flour
1 tablespoon sugar	1 egg yolk, beaten
1/2 cup shortening	Sesame seed or coarse salt

Dissolve yeast in water in bowl. Add sugar, shortening, salt and half the flour; beat until smooth. Mix in remaining flour. Knead on floured surface for 5 minutes or until smooth. Place in greased bowl, turning to grease surface. Let rise, covered, for 1 hour or until doubled in bulk. Divide dough into 2 portions. Cut each into 24 pieces. Roll each piece into 8-inch rope on floured surface. Place 1 inch apart on greased baking sheet. Brush with egg yolk. Sprinkle with sesame seed or salt. Bake at 400° F. for 25 minutes. Yield: 4 dozen.

ONION AND GARLIC CORN BREAD
(PANE DI GRANTURCO CON CIPOLLE ED AGLI)

1 onion, chopped	16 ounces yellow cornmeal
1 clove of garlic, minced	1/2 cup Parmesan cheese
1/2 cup olive oil	1 cup raisins
4 cups hot water	1/2 cup pine nuts
2 teaspoons salt	1/2 cup chopped walnuts

Sauté onion and garlic in olive oil in saucepan. Stir in hot water and salt. Bring to a boil. Add cornmeal gradually, stirring until smooth; remove from heat. Stir in remaining ingredients. Pour into greased baking pan. Bake at 350° F. for 30 minutes. Serve immediately. Yield: 6 servings.

MOZZARELLA CHEESE ROLLS

2 cups sifted flour	3 tablespoons shortening
2 teaspoons baking powder	2/3 cup milk
1 teaspoon salt	4 ounces mozzarella cheese

Sift flour, baking powder and salt into bowl. Cut in shortening until crumbly. Stir in milk to form a soft dough. Knead on floured surface for 1 minute. Roll 1/4 inch thick. Cut with biscuit cutter. Cut cheese into 1/4-inch strips. Place 1 strip on each circle. Fold dough over to enclose cheese; seal edges. Place close together on baking sheet. Bake at 450° F. for 10 minutes. Yield: 1 dozen.

CHRISTMAS BREAD

1 package yeast	1/2 cup butter, softened
1/4 cup lukewarm water	1 teaspoon salt
1/2 cup flour	4 cups flour
1/2 cup lukewarm water	1 egg
3 tablespoons honey	1 1/2 cups flour
3/4 cup sugar	1/2 cup raisins
3 tablespoons lukewarm water	1/2 cup chopped candied fruit
4 egg yolks	1/2 cup chopped nuts

Dissolve yeast in 1/4 cup lukewarm water. Add 1/2 cup flour and 1/2 cup lukewarm water. Let rise, covered, in warm place for 1 hour. Combine honey, sugar, 3 tablespoons lukewarm water, egg yolks, butter and salt in mixer bowl; mix well. Add to yeast mixture; mix well. Mix in 4 cups flour. Place on floured surface; make hole in center of dough. Break egg into hole. Knead for 1 minute. Add remaining 1 1/2 cups flour. Knead for 5 minutes. Knead in raisins, candied fruit and nuts. Place in greased bowl, turning to grease surface. Let rise, covered, for 1 1/2 hours or until doubled in bulk. Shape into 2 round loaves. Place on baking sheet. Let rise for 4 to 6 hours. Cut cross in top of each loaf. Bake at 350° F. for 10 minutes. Recut crosses on tops of loaves. Bake for 30 to 35 minutes longer. Cool on wire rack. Yield: 2 loaves.

PANE DI NATALE

1 confezione di lievito di birra	1/2 tazza di burro ammorbidito
1/4 di tazza di acqua tiepida	1 cucchiaino di sale
1/2 tazza di farina	4 tazze di farina
1/2 tazza di acqua tiepida	1 uovo
3 cucchiai di miele	1 tazza e 1/2 di farina
3/4 di tazza di zucchero	1/2 tazza di uvetta sultanina
3 cucchiai di acqua tiepida	1/2 tazza di frutta candita tritata
4 tuorli d'uovo	1/2 tazza di noci tritate

Scogliere il lievito in un 1/4 di tazza di acqua tiepida. Aggiungere 1/2 tazza di farina e 1/2 di tazza di acqua tiepida. Lasciare in un luogo tiepido a lievitare per 1 ora. Mescolare in una ciotola: miele, zucchero, 3 cucchiai di acqua teipida, i tuorli d'uovo, burro e sale. Aggiungere questa miscela al lievito e mescolare accuratamente. Aggiungere 4 tazze di farina. Sistemare su una superficie infarinata; creare una depressione al centro della pagnottella e rompervi l'uovo. Impastare per 1 minuto. Aggiungere la tazza e mezza di farina rimasta. Impastare per 5 minuti. Aggiungere l'uvetta, i canditi e le noci. Sistemare la pagnottella in una ciotola unta, ungendola esternamente. Metterla in un luogo tiepido a lievitare, coperta, per 1 ora e mezza, fino a quando raddoppia di volume. Formare due pagnottelle separate. Sistemarle sulla lastra del forno. Lasciarle lievitare, coperte, per 4-6 ore. Fare un taglio a croce su ogni pagnottella. Cuocere in forno a 350° F. per 10 minuti. Fare di nuovo un taglio a croce su ogni pagnottella. Cuocere per altri 30-35 minuti. Lasciarle intiepidire su una graticola.

MACAROONS AMARETTI

2 cups almonds	1 cup sugar
1/4 teaspoon almond extract	2 egg whites

Process almonds in blender until finely ground. Combine with almond extract and half the sugar in bowl. Beat egg whites in mixer bowl until soft peaks form. Add remaining 1/2 cup sugar, beating constantly until stiff peaks form. Fold in almond mixture. Shape into balls. Place on greased baking sheet; press lightly to flatten. Bake at 350° F. for 8 to 10 minutes or until light brown. Cool on wire rack. Yield: 3 dozen.

NEAPOLITAN NOUGAT (TORRONE ALLA NAPOLETANA)

2 cups sugar	1/2 cup finely chopped
1/3 cup corn syrup	hazelnuts
1 cup water	1/2 cup finely chopped candied
4 egg whites, stiffly beaten	cherries
1 teaspoon vanilla extract	

Combine half the sugar, half the corn syrup and half the water in saucepan. Cook over low heat until sugar is completely dissolved, stirring constantly. Cook, covered, over medium heat for 2 to 3 minutes or until steam washes sugar crystals from side of pan. Cook, uncovered, over high heat to 240° to 248° on candy thermometer, firm-ball stage. Remove from heat. Pour very gradually over egg whites, beating constantly. Combine remaining sugar, corn syrup and water in clean saucepan. Cook to firm-ball stage, following directions for first mixture. Add to egg white mixture gradually, beating constantly. Cool. Add vanilla, hazelnuts and cherries. Pour into 2 buttered 8 x 8-inch dishes. Let stand overnight. Cut into 1 x 2-inch pieces. Wrap individually in waxed paper. Yield: 32 pieces.

NEAPOLITAN TORTE

1 cup sifted cake flour	2 tablespoons cherry juice
1/4 teaspoon salt	1 tablespoon vinegar
4 egg whites	1/2 cup chopped almonds
1 cup sugar	2 teaspoons almond extract
4 egg yolks	2 tablespoons confectioners'
25 maraschino cherries,	sugar
chopped	

Sift flour and salt together 3 times. Set aside. Beat egg whites at high speed in mixer bowl until soft peaks form. Add sugar gradually, beating constantly until stiff peaks form. Beat egg yolks in mixer bowl until thick and lemon-colored. Fold gently into egg whites. Fold in cherries, cherry juice, vinegar, almonds and almond extract. Fold in flour mixture. Spoon into greased 9 x 9-inch cake pan lined with waxed paper. Bake at 350° F. for 35 minutes or until golden brown. Remove to wire rack to cool. Remove waxed paper. Dust with confectioners' sugar. Yield: 6 servings.

TORTA NAPOLETANA

1 tazza di farina setacciata per	2 cucchiai di succo di ciliege
torte	1 cucchiaio di aceto
1/4 di cucchiaino di sale	1/2 tazza di mandorle tritate
4 albumi d'uovo	2 cucchiaini di estratto di
1 tazza di zucchero	mandorle
4 tuorli d'uovo	2 cucchiai di zucchero a velo
25 ciliege al maraschino tritate	

Setacciare insieme la farina ed il sale per 3 volte. Mettere da parte. Montare a neve gli albumi in una ciotola. Aggiungere lentamente lo zucchero, senza smettere di mescolare. Sbattere i tuorli d'uovo in una ciotola fino ad ottenere un composto omogeneo e di color limone. Mescolare delicatamente insieme agli albumi. Aggiungere ciliege, succo di ciliege, aceto, mandorle ed estratto di mandorle. Versare in una tortiera (9 x 9 pollici), foderata con carta oleata. Cuocere in forno a 350° F. per 25 minuti o fino a quando si presenta ben dorata. Sformare il dolce e lasciarlo raffreddare su una graticola. Togliere la carta oleata. Spolverizzare con lo zucchero a velo.

SPUMONI

5 egg yolks, lightly beaten
3/4 cup sugar
2 cups cold milk
1 1/2 teaspoons vanilla extract
1 cup whipping cream, whipped

2 tablespoons chopped candied orange peel
10 maraschino cherries, chopped
10 slivered blanched almonds

Combine egg yolks, sugar and milk in double boiler. Cook over simmering water for 8 minutes or until thickened. Cool. Add vanilla. Pour into freezer tray. Freeze until slushy. Spoon into chilled bowl. Beat just until smooth. Fold in remaining ingredients. Spoon into mold. Freeze, covered, for 3 hours or until firm. Unmold onto serving dish. Serve immediately. Yield: 6 servings.

TORTONI PARFAITS

1 egg yolk
6 tablespoons confectioners' sugar
3/4 cup whipping cream, whipped

1 1/2 teaspoons vanilla extract
1 egg white
1 cup crushed macaroons or almond cookies

Beat egg yolk and confectioners' sugar in mixer bowl until thick and lemon-colored. Fold in whipped cream and vanilla. Beat egg white in bowl until stiff peaks form. Fold gently into whipped cream mixture. Alternate layers of cookie crumbs and whipped cream mixture in parfait glasses until all ingredients are used. Freeze for 3 hours or until firm. Yield: 4 to 6 servings.

ZABAGLIONE

8 egg yolks, at room temperature
2/3 cup sugar

1 cup grape juice or Marsala, at room temperature

Combine egg yolks and sugar in top of double boiler. Beat with wire whisk until thick. Place over hot water. Add grape juice gradually, beating constantly. Cook until smooth and of the consistency of heavy sour cream, beating constantly. Serve warm or chilled over cake or fresh fruit. Yield: 6 to 8 servings.

COCINA
LATINOAMERICANA
LATIN AMERICA

CINNAMON TEA

5 cinnamon sticks   6 tea bags
8 cups water   1 cup sugar

Combine cinnamon sticks and water in large saucepan. Boil for 3 minutes; remove from heat. Add tea bags. Let steep for 10 minutes; remove cinnamon sticks and tea bags. Stir in sugar. Heat just to serving temperature. Serve in cups with cinnamon sticks for stirrers. Yield: 10 servings.

HOT TEA MIX

2 cups instant orange drink   2 cups sugar
1 cup unsweetened $1/2$ teaspoon cinnamon
   lemon-flavored instant tea $1/2$ teaspoon ground cloves

Combine all ingredients in large bowl; mix well. Store in airtight container. Stir 2 teaspoons tea mix into 1 cup boiling water for each serving.

TÉ RUSO

2 tazas de polvo de bebida de $1/2$ cucharadita de canela en
   naranja   polvo
1 taza de té instantáneo sabor $1/2$ cucharadita de clavo de
   limón, sin azúcar   olor en polvo
2 tazas de azúcar

Mezcle bien todos los ingredientes en una vasija grande. Guarde en un recipiente hermético. Use 2 cucharaditas de esta mexcla por cada taza de agua hirviendo.

HOT CHOCOLATE — Mexico

4 ounces sweet chocolate
1 cup hot water
5 1/2 cups milk
1/2 cup cream

1 tablespoon cinnamon
1/8 teaspoon nutmeg
1 teaspoon vanilla extract

Melt chocolate with hot water in double boiler. Combine milk, cream and spices in saucepan; mix well. Heat just to the simmering point, stirring occasionally; remove from heat. Add chocolate mixture and vanilla; beat until smooth. Pour into cups. Serve with cinnamon stick stirrers. Yield: 6 servings.

HOT MOCHA CHOCOLATE (CHOCÁ) — Brazil

2 1/2 cups milk
3 ounces semisweet chocolate
3/4 cup strong hot coffee

Sugar to taste
Whipped cream

Bring milk to the simmering point in saucepan. Add chocolate, stirring until melted. Stir in coffee and sugar to taste. Pour into cups. Spoon dollop of whipped cream onto each cup. Yield: 4 cups.

ORANGE SLUSH (BATIDA DE LARANJA) — Brazil

6 cups orange juice
3 bananas

10 maraschino cherries
1 cup crushed ice

Combine orange juice, bananas and cherries in blender. Add ice; process until slushy. Pour into glasses. Yield: 8 servings.

PINEAPPLE PUNCH (PONCHE DE PIÑA) — Mexico

1 cup sugar
1 1/2 cups water
4 cinnamon sticks
12 cloves

1 46-ounce can pineapple juice
1 1/2 cups orange juice
1/2 cup lemon juice

Combine sugar, water, cinnamon and cloves in saucepan. Simmer for 30 minutes. Strain into pitcher. Add juices. Chill until serving time. Serve over ice or frozen pineapple chunks in glasses or punch cups. Yield: 2 quarts.

GUACAMOLE

4 medium avocados, peeled,
   mashed
1 medium tomato, chopped
1/4 cup chopped onion
1 teaspoon lemon juice

1/2 teaspoon salt
1/2 teaspoon pepper
1/2 teaspoon Tabasco sauce
1/4 cup mayonnaise
1 head lettuce, shredded

Combine avocado, tomato, onion, lemon juice, salt, pepper, Tabasco sauce and mayonnaise in bowl; mix well. Place lettuce on serving plates. Spoon avocado mixture over lettuce. Yield: 6 servings.

GUACAMOLE

4 aguacates medianos, pelados
   y machacados
1 tomate mediano, picado
1/4 taza de cebolla picada
1 cucharadita de jugo de limón
1/2 cucharadita de sal

1/2 cucharadita de pimienta
1/2 cucharadita de salsa
   Tabasco
1/4 taza mayonesa
1 lechuga picada

Se combinen los aguacates, tomate, cebolla, jugo de limón, sal, pimienta, salsa Tabasco y mayonesa y se mezcla todo bien. Acomode la lechuga en 6 platos. Con una cuchara, ponga la mezcla de aguacate encima de la lechuga.

LITTLE CHICKEN LEGS (COXINHAS) — Mexico

1 3-pound chicken, cut up	1/8 teaspoon pepper
3 cups water	1 cup milk
1 teaspoon salt	2 egg yolks
2 tablespoons butter	1 1/2 cups bread crumbs
3/4 cup rice flour	1 egg, beaten
1 teaspoon salt	Oil for deep frying

Combine chicken, water and 1 teaspoon salt in 4-quart saucepan. Simmer for 1 hour or until chicken is tender. Drain, reserving 1 cup broth. Chop chicken, discarding skin and bones. Blend butter, rice flour, 1 teaspoon salt and pepper in saucepan. Stir in reserved broth and milk. Cook until thickened, stirring constantly. Beat egg yolks in bowl. Stir a small amount of hot mixture into egg yolks; stir egg yolks into hot mixture. Cook for 2 minutes, stirring constantly. Stir in chicken. Chill in refrigerator. Shape by 2 tablespoonfuls to resemble chicken legs. Roll in bread crumbs, dip in beaten egg, then roll again in crumbs. Insert wooden skewer into each. Deep-fry in 375° oil for 3 minutes or until golden brown. Drain on paper towel. Purchase rice flour in specialty shop or process brown rice in blender until finely ground. Yield: 30 servings.

CHICKEN LIVERS IN WINE SAUCE — Mexico

1 pound chicken livers	2 tablespoons chopped parsley
2 tablespoons butter	1/4 teaspoon salt
1/4 cup dry Sherry	1/8 teaspoon pepper
1 tablespoon lemon juice	

Cut chicken livers into bite-sized pieces. Sauté in butter in skillet over medium heat for 5 minutes. Add remaining ingredients; mix well. Cook until heated through. Serve on toast rounds or in chafing dish.

CODFISH APPETIZERS — (BOLINHOS DE BACALHAU)

8 ounces salt codfish
1 1/2 cups sliced peeled potatoes
1/4 cup onion
2 tablespoons chopped parsley
Pepper to taste

1 tablespoon butter
2 tablespoons flour
1 egg
Oil for deep frying

Combine codfish with water to cover in bowl; cover. Soak for 12 hours, changing water once. Drain and chop fish. Cook potatoes in water in saucepan for 20 minutes or until tender; drain. Sauté codfish, onion, parsley and pepper in butter in skillet. Combine mixture with potatoes, flour and egg in mixer bowl; beat until smooth. Chill for 1 hour or longer. Shape into small balls. Deep-fry a few at a time in hot oil until golden, turning once. Drain on paper towel.
Yield: 40 appetizers.

CHILI CON QUESO DIP

1 pound Velveeta cheese
1 roll garlic cheese
1 roll jalapeño cheese

8 ounces cream cheese
1/2 cup jalapeño chili sauce
1 can evaporated milk

Chop all cheeses. Combine with chili sauce and evaporated milk in heavy saucepan. Cook over low heat until cheese is melted, stirring to mix well. Serve with corn chips or tortilla chips.

MEAT AND CHEESE DIP

2 pounds Velveeta cheese,
  chopped
1   16-ounce jar Cheez Whiz
1 pound Monterey Jack
  cheese, shredded
1 pound chopped cooked
  chicken

1 pound chopped cooked roast
  beef
2 green onions, chopped
1 can cream of chicken soup
1 teaspoon garlic powder
1/2 teaspoon chili powder

Combine all ingredients in saucepan. Cook over low heat until cheeses are melted, stirring to mix well. Serve warm with tortilla chips.

BAKED EMPANADAS (EMPANADAS DE HORNO) — Mexico

8 ounces ground beef
1/2 cup finely chopped onion
1 clove of garlic, minced
1/4 teaspoon salt
1/8 teaspoon cumin
Pepper to taste
1 1/2 teaspoons flour

1/2 cup water
1/2 cup milk
1/3 cup shortening
1 teaspoon salt
2 cups flour
2 hard-boiled eggs, chopped

Brown ground beef with onion and garlic in skillet, stirring until ground beef is crumbly; drain. Stir in 1/4 teaspoon salt, cumin and pepper. Blend 1 1/2 teaspoons flour with water. Add to ground beef mixture. Cook until thickened, stirring constantly. Set aside. Combine milk, shortening and 1 teaspoon salt in saucepan. Heat until shortening is melted, stirring to blend well. Place 2 cups flour in bowl; make well in center. Add shortening mixture; mix to form dough. Knead on floured surface until smooth. Roll thin; cut into 2 1/2-inch circles. Spoon meat filling onto half the circles. Sprinkle with chopped egg. Cut out centers of remaining circles with 1-inch cutter. Place circles over filling. Seal edges. Place on baking sheet. Bake at 400° F. for 15 minutes.

GUACAMOLE DIP — Mexico

1 cup mashed avocado
2 tablespoons grated onion
2 to 4 tablespoons chopped
   green chilies

1/4 teaspoon crushed garlic
1/2 teaspoon salt
1/4 teaspoon pepper

Combine avocado with remaining ingredients in bowl; mix well. Chill in refrigerator. Serve with tostados. Yield: 1 1/2 cups.

HOT BEAN DIP

2 cans bean dip
1/2 cup sour cream
4 ounces cream cheese,
   softened

1/2 cup chopped green onions
Shredded Cheddar cheese
Shredded Monterey cheese

Combine bean dip, sour cream, cream cheese and green onions in bowl; mix well. Spread in 9-inch pie plate. Top with Cheddar and Monterey Jack cheeses. Bake at 350° F. for 30 minutes. Serve with tortilla chips. Yield: 6 servings.

SEVICHE — Mexico

1 pound white saltwater fish
   fillets
6 to 8 large limes
1/2 medium onion, chopped

1 medium tomato, chopped
1/4 cup catsup
1 teaspoon horseradish

Chop fish into 1/4-inch pieces. Place in dish. Squeeze lime juice over fish. Chill for 4 hours. Add onion and tomato. Mix catsup and horseradish in small bowl. Mix with fish. Chill for 1 hour. Yield: 12 servings.

HEARTS OF PALM TURNOVERS
(PASTELS PALMITO) — Mexico

2 tablespoons butter
2 tablespoons flour
Pepper to taste
1/2 cup milk

3/4 cup chopped drained hearts
   of palm
2 tablespoons chopped parsley
1 recipe 2-crust pie pastry

Melt butter in saucepan. Blend in flour and pepper. Add milk. Cook until thickened, stirring constantly. Add hearts of palm and parsley. Roll pastry 1/16 inch thick on floured surface. Cut into sixteen 4-inch circles. Place 1 tablespoon filling on each circle. Fold pastry to enclose filling. Moisten edges; press to seal. Place on baking sheet. Bake at 375° F. for 20 to 25 minutes or until brown. Yield: 16 servings.

BLACK BEAN SOUP (SOPA DE CARAOTAS NEGRAS)

1 cup dried black beans
1 leek, sliced
1 onion, chopped
1 clove of garlic, crushed
2 tablespoons oil

6 cups beef broth
1 tablespoon brown sugar
1/2 teaspoon salt
2 tablespoons butter
1 cup toasted croutons

Soak beans in water to cover in bowl overnight; drain. Combine with fresh water to cover by 1 inch in saucepan. Bring to a boil; reduce heat. Simmer, covered, for 2 to 3 hours or until beans are tender. Sauté leek, onion and garlic in oil in saucepan until golden. Add broth, brown sugar and salt. Simmer for 10 minutes. Drain beans; press through sieve into broth. Stir in butter. Simmer for 2 minutes. Ladle into soup bowls. Sprinkle with croutons. Yield: 6 servings.

BEEF SOUP (CAZUELA DE VACA)

2 pounds flank steak
1 tablespoon oil
6 cups water
1 tablespoon salt
4 potatoes, peeled, cut into
  quarters
2 ears of corn, cut into quarters
2 carrots, cut into 1-inch pieces
1 cup sliced green beans
2 onions, cut into quarters

8 ounces winter squash, cut
  into 8 pieces
1/4 cup chopped celery leaves
2 cloves of garlic, minced
1/4 cup chopped parsley
1/4 cup long grain rice
1/4 teaspoon white pepper
1/8 teaspoon crushed dried
  chilies

Cut steak into 8 portions. Brown 1/2 at a time in hot oil in heavy saucepan. Add water and salt. Bring to a boil; reduce heat. Simmer, covered, for 1 hour and 15 minutes or until almost tender. Add remaining ingredients. Simmer, covered, for 30 minutes or until vegetables are tender. Yield: 8 servings.

PUMPKIN SOUP (SOPA DE CALABEZA)

1 pound lean beef short ribs
Oil
4 cups water
3 cups chopped peeled
  pumpkin
1 potato, peeled, chopped

1 large carrot, chopped
1 medium onion, chopped
1 1/2 teaspoons salt
1/4 teaspoon white pepper

Brown short ribs in heavy saucepan, adding a small amount of oil if necessary. Add water. Bring to a boil; reduce heat. Simmer, covered, for 1 hour. Remove ribs from broth; cool. Cut meat from bones; return meat to broth. Add remaining ingredients. Simmer, covered, over medium heat for 45 minutes. Process 1/2 at a time in blender until smooth. Return to saucepan. Cook until heated through. Ladle into soup bowls. Garnish with cream if desired. Yield: 6 servings.

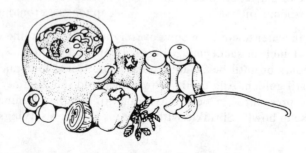

TRIPE STEW - El Salvador

6 pounds tripe	1 onion
4 bananas	4 tomatoes
6 hot peppers	6 cups cut green beans
4 squash	1 tablespoon chopped garlic
1 cabbage	1 tablespoon cumin

Cook tripe in water to cover in saucepan until tender. Chop bananas, hot peppers, squash, cabbage, onion and tomatoes. Add all ingredients to saucepan. Simmer for 1 hour. Yield: 10 servings.

SOPA DE MENUDO — El Salvador

6 libras de menudo	4 tomates
4 plátanos	6 tazas de frijoles verdes
6 chiles picantes	(ejotes)
4 calabacitas	1 cucharada de ajo picado
1 repollo	1 cucharada de comino en
1 cebolla	polvo

Hierva el menudo en agua de cubrir en una olla. Corte los plátanos, chiles, calabacitas, repollo, cebolla, tomates y frijoles verdes. Agréguelo todo a la olla con el ajo y el comino en polvo. Cocine 1 hora.

VEGETABLE AND BEEF SOUP
(SOPA DE VERDURA Y CARNE)

1 1/2 pounds boneless lean beef	2 cups chopped sweet potatoes
2 tablespoons oil	1 cup chopped winter squash
1 small onion, chopped	1 tomato, peeled, chopped
1 clove of garlic, minced	2 teaspoons salt
1 teaspoon paprika	1/4 teaspoon white pepper
3 cups water	1 8-ounce can corn
2 cups chopped potatoes	2 cups torn fresh spinach

Cut beef into 1/2-inch cubes. Brown half the beef in hot oil in saucepan; remove with slotted spoon. Brown remaining beef with onion, garlic and paprika. Simmer beef and water, covered, in saucepan for 1 1/4 hours. Add next 6 ingredients and undrained corn. Simmer, covered, for 20 minutes or until vegetables are tender. Stir in spinach. Simmer for 3 to 5 minutes longer. Yield: 6 servings.

STEW (PUCHERO CRIOLLO)

1 pound beef short ribs
2 ounces lean salt pork, sliced
5 cups water
1 1/2 teaspoons salt
1/8 teaspoon pepper
1 3-pound chicken, cut up
3 carrots, chopped
3 potatoes, chopped

1 cup chopped winter squash
3 tomatoes, chopped
1/2 head cabbage, cut into
  wedges
1/2 cup chopped green pepper
3 tablespoons chopped parsley
1 clove of garlic, minced

Combine short ribs, salt pork, water, salt and pepper in heavy 5-quart saucepan. Bring to a boil; reduce heat. Simmer, covered, for 1 hour. Add chicken. Simmer, covered, for 20 minutes. Add remaining ingredients. Simmer, covered, for 20 minutes longer or until vegetables are tender. Cool. Chill overnight. Skim. Bring to a boil. Remove beef and vegetables to platter with slotted spoon. Serve with broth. Yield: 6 servings.

FISH SOUP (CALDILLO DE PESCADO)

1 cup chopped onion
1 clove of garlic, minced
2 tablespoons olive oil
2 cups water
1 1/2 cups chopped potato
1 1/2 cups chopped tomato

1/2 cup dry white wine
1/2 teaspoon salt
Pepper to taste
1 1/2 pounds fish fillets
2 egg yolks
2 tablespoons chopped parsley

Sauté onion and garlic in olive oil in saucepan. Stir in water, potato, tomato, wine, salt and pepper. Bring to a boil; reduce heat. Simmer, covered, for 20 minutes. Cut fish into 3/4-inch pieces. Add to soup. Simmer, covered, for 10 minutes or until fish flakes easily. Beat egg yolks in bowl. Add a small amount of hot broth to egg yolks; stir egg yolks into soup. Cook over low heat until thickened. Stir in parsley. Yield: 6 to 8 servings.

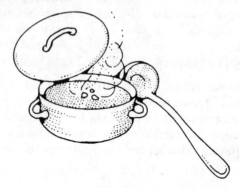

CHICKEN SALAD

4 cups chopped cooked chicken
1 cup chopped celery
1 cup seedless green grapes,
   cut into halves
1 teaspoon salt

1/4 teaspoon pepper
3/4 cup mayonnaise
1/4 cup sour cream
1 cup chopped salted peanuts

Combine chicken, celery, grapes, salt and pepper in large bowl. Blend mayonnaise and sour cream in small bowl. Add to chicken mixture; mix well. Chill in refrigerator for several hours. Add peanuts at serving time; mix lightly. Yield: 8 to 10 servings.

ENSALADA DE POLLO

4 tazas de pollo cocido, picado
1 taza de apio picado
1 taza de uvas verdes sin
   semillas, partidas
1 cucharadita de sal

1/4 cucharadita de pimienta
3/4 taza de mayonesa
1/4 taza de crema agria
1 taza de cacahuates salados
   picados

Se combinen el pollo, apio, uvas, sal y pimiento en una vasija grande. Aparte se mezcla la mayonesa con la crema agria, y luego se añade a la mezcla de pollo, mezclándose todo bien. Se refrigera por varias horas. Se añaden los cacahuates antes de servir esta ensalada, y se revuelve un poco.

CALYPSO SALAD — Haiti

2 avocados
1 tablespoon lemon juice
1 7-ounce can tuna
1/2 cup chopped celery
2 tablespoons chopped pimento

2 tablespoons mayonnaise
Salt and pepper to taste
1/4 cup bread crumbs
1 tablespoon melted butter

Cut unpeeled avocados into halves lengthwise. Brush with lemon juice. Combine tuna, celery, pimento, mayonnaise, salt and pepper in bowl; mix well. Spoon into avocado halves. Toss bread crumbs with melted butter in bowl. Sprinkle over salads. Broil just until golden brown. Serve immediately. Yield: 4 servings.

CHRISTMAS SALAD

1 head lettuce
8 cooked beets, sliced
4 oranges, peeled, sliced
4 bananas, sliced
1 pineapple, peeled, sliced

4 apples, sliced
1 cup cubed cheese
1 cup chopped peanuts
1/2 cup oil
1/4 cup red wine vinegar

Chop lettuce; place in shallow salad bowl. Layer beets, oranges, bananas, pineapple, apples, cheese and peanuts over lettuce. Pour oil and vinegar over salad at serving time. Yield: 8 servings.

ENSALADA DE NAVIDAD

1 cabeza de lechuga verde
8 remolachas cocidas, en
   rebanadas
4 naranjas peladas, en
   rebanadas
4 plátanos, en rebanadas
1 piña pelada, en rebanadas

4 manzanas, en rebanadas
1 taza de queso en cubitos
1 taza de cacahuates picados
1/2 taza de aceite
1/4 taza de vinagre de vino
   tinto

Corte la lechuga y póngala sobre una fuente. Ponga las remolachas, las naranjas, los plátanos, la piña, las manzanas, el queso y los cacahuates encima de la lechuga. Rocíe con aceite y vinagre a la hora de comer.

SAN JUAN SALAD — Puerto Rico

1 cup cooked tiny beets
5 cups sliced cooked potatoes
2 cups cooked cut green beans
1/2 cup sliced celery
1/2 cup sliced green onions
1/2 cup sliced radishes

1 teaspoon salt
1/2 teaspoon cracked pepper
1/2 cup mayonnaise
1/4 cup sour cream
1 cup French dressing
3 tablespoons horseradish

Combine vegetables, salt and pepper in salad bowl. Mix mayonnaise, sour cream, French dressing and horseradish in bowl. Add to salad; toss lightly to mix. Chill until serving time. Yield: 8 to 10 servings.

HAM SALAD (ENSALADA DE JAMÓN)

1 cauliflower
3 tablespoons olive oil
1 tablespoon wine vinegar
1 teaspoon salt
Pepper to taste
1 cup chopped cooked ham

1/4 cup minced parsley
1/2 cup mayonnaise
2 tablespoons light cream
1 teaspoon lime juice
1 avocado

Break cauliflower into flowerets. Cook in salted water in saucepan until tender-crisp; drain. Mix olive oil, vinegar, salt and pepper in bowl. Add cauliflower. Chill in refrigerator. Add next 5 ingredients; mix lightly. Slice avocado over salad. Yield: 6 servings.

BEEF CARNITAS

1 avocado, chopped
1 tomato, chopped
1/2 onion, finely chopped
1/4 cup chopped green chilies
1 teaspoon lemon juice
1/2 teaspoon cumin
1/2 teaspoon salt

8 corn tortillas
1 pound boneless beef chuck
1 clove of garlic, minced
1 tablespoon oil
1/2 cup chili sauce
Hot pepper sauce

Combine avocado, tomato, onion, chilies, lemon juice, cumin and salt in bowl. Set aside. Sprinkle tortillas lightly with water. Wrap in foil. Heat in 350° F.-oven for 10 to 15 minutes or until heated through. Cut beef into small cubes. Brown beef with garlic in hot oil in skillet. Stir in chili sauce and pepper sauce. Simmer until heated through. Spoon beef mixture and avocado mixture onto hot tortillas, folding to enclose filling. Yield: 4 servings.

Photograph for this recipe on page 68.

STEAK WITH BLACK BEANS, RICE AND PLANTAINS

2 pounds sirloin steak,
  1/2 inch thick
1 cup chopped onion
1 teaspoon minced garlic
1/3 cup olive oil

6 medium tomatoes, peeled,
  chopped
1/2 teaspoon cumin
1 teaspoon salt

Broil steak 4 inches from heat source for 5 minutes on each side or until medium-rare. Cut into 1/4 x 1/2-inch strips. Sauté onion and garlic in olive oil in 12-inch skillet for 5 minutes. Add tomatoes, cumin and salt. Simmer for 30 minutes or until thick, stirring occasionally. Add beef. Simmer until heated through. Spoon into center of large platter. Mound beans and rice around beef. Top with slices of plantain. Serve immediately. Yield: 4 to 6 servings.

Black Beans

1 1/2 cups dried black beans
5 cups cold water
1/2 cup chopped green pepper
2 tablespoons chopped onion

1/2 teaspoon chopped garlic
2 tablespoons olive oil
3 sprigs fresh cilantro

Bring beans and water to a boil in heavy 5-quart saucepan; reduce heat. Simmer for 2 hours. Sauté green pepper, onion and garlic in olive oil in heavy 10-inch skillet for 3 minutes. Add to beans. Add cilantro. Simmer for 15 minutes. Discard cilantro.

Rice

1/2 large onion
1/2 large green pepper
1/4 cup olive oil

2 cups long grain rice
4 cups boiling water
2 teaspoons salt

Sauté onion and green pepper halves in olive oil in heavy 4-quart saucepan for 5 minutes. Add rice. Sauté for 3 minutes. Add water and salt. Bring to a boil; reduce heat. Simmer, covered, for 20 minutes or until rice is tender and liquid is absorbed. Discard onion and green pepper.

Plantains

2 large plantains, sliced

1/2 cup oil

Cook plantains in oil in skillet for 2 to 3 minutes on each side or until tender and golden brown.

BAKED FAJITAS (FAJITAS AL HORNO)

3 to 5 pounds beef skirt
Salt and pepper to taste
1/3 cup water
1 tablespoon vinegar

1 6-ounce can Ro-Tel tomatoes
   with chilies
1 or 2 jalapeño peppers, sliced

Sprinkle beef with salt and pepper. Cut into 4 pieces. Combine with water and vinegar in baking dish. Pour tomatoes over top. Top with jalapeño peppers. Bake at 350° F. for 45 to 60 minutes. Slice beef into thin strips. Return to baking dish. Bake for 30 minutes longer. May refrigerate, skim and reheat.
Yield: 4 to 6 servings.

STEAKS IN BEER SAUCE (BIFES COM CERVEJA) — Brazil

1 cup sliced onions
2 tablespoons tomato paste
1 tablespoon flour
1 cup light beer

1 pound sirloin steak
Salt and pepper to taste
2 tablespoons butter

Combine onions, tomato paste, flour and beer in bowl; mix well. Let stand for 2 hours. Slice steak into 1/2-inch strips. Sprinkle with salt and pepper. Sauté in butter in skillet. Place in greased baking dish. Pour beer mixture over beef. Bake, covered, at 375° F. for 30 minutes. Remove cover. Bake for 20 minutes or until sauce is thickened to desired consistency. Yield: 3 to 4 servings.

CHILAQUILLES — Mexico

12 corn tortillas
Oil for frying
1 clove of garlic, chopped
1 small green chili, chopped
1 pound ground beef
1/2 pound pork, diced

2 cups chopped tomatoes
3 cups water
1 tablespoon salt
Shredded cheese
10 to 15 ripe olives

Cut tortillas into 1-inch squares. Fry in hot oil in saucepan; drain. Sauté garlic and chili in saucepan. Add beef and pork. Cook until meat is tender, stirring frequently. Add tomatoes, water, salt and fried tortillas. Cook for 30 minutes. Pour into baking dish. Top with cheese and olives. Bake at 350° F. for 15 minutes.
Yield: 6 servings.

BEEF AND CORN CASSEROLE

1/2 cup chopped onion	1/3 cup sliced green olives
1/2 cup chopped green pepper	Salt and pepper to taste
1 tablespoon butter	1 hard-boiled egg
1 pound ground beef	1 egg, separated
2 tablespoons chopped parsley	1 12-ounce can cream-style
1/2 cup raisins	corn

Sauté onion and green pepper in butter until lightly browned. Add ground beef. Cook until beef is crumbly, stirring constantly; drain. Add parsley, raisins, olives, salt and pepper. Cook until heated through. Pour into baking dish. Sprinkle with hard-boiled egg. Combine egg yolk and corn in bowl; mix well. Beat egg white in bowl until stiff peaks form. Fold into corn mixture. Spoon over casserole. Bake at 375° F. for 30 minutes or until golden. Yield: 6 servings.

CHILI CASSEROLE - Mexico

1 pound ground beef	1 cup shredded Cheddar cheese
1 15-ounce can enchilada sauce	1 1/2 cups sour cream
1 8-ounce can tomato sauce	1/2 cup shredded Cheddar
1 16-ounce can chili beans	cheese
1 tablespoon minced onion	

Brown ground beef in skillet, stirring until crumbly; drain. Stir in enchilada sauce, tomato sauce, beans, onion and 1 cup cheese; mix well. Spoon into 9 x 13-inch baking dish. Bake at 350° F. for 20 to 25 minutes. Spread sour cream on top. Sprinkle with 1/2 cup cheese. Bake for 4 minutes longer. Serve over chips, lettuce and tomato. Yield: 6 servings.

CORN AND TAMALE CASSEROLE

1 16-ounce can whole kernel corn, drained	Salt and pepper to taste
1 16-ounce can cream-style corn	2 16-ounce cans tamales

Combine corn and cream-style corn in bowl; mix well. Spread half the mixture in shallow baking dish. Season to taste. Remove wrapping from tamales. Arrange over corn. Top with remaining corn mixture. Bake at 375° F. for 30 minutes or until bubbly. Yield: 4 servings.

BEEF AND CORN PIE (PASTEL DE CHOCLO) — Mexico

1 pound ground beef
1 cup chopped onion
1/4 cup beef broth
3/4 teaspoon salt
1/2 teaspoon cumin
1/4 teaspoon chili peppers
1/8 teaspoon marjoram
1/4 teaspoon pepper
2 teaspoons flour
3 tablespoons cold water

4 ears of fresh corn
1 cup milk
1 teaspoon sugar
1/4 teaspoon basil
1/2 teaspoon salt
2 eggs, separated
1/2 cup chopped black olives
1/4 cup raisins
1 hard-boiled egg, sliced
1 tablespoon sugar

Brown ground beef with onion in skillet; drain. Stir in next 6 ingredients. Simmer, covered, for 30 minutes. Blend flour and water in cup. Stir into ground beef mixture. Cook until thickened, stirring constantly. Keep warm. Cut off tips of kernels of corn. Scrape out remaining corn pulp with knife; measure 2 cups corn. Combine with milk, 1 teaspoon sugar, basil and 1/2 teaspoon salt in saucepan. Simmer, covered, for 10 minutes. Beat egg yolks in bowl. Stir a small amount of hot corn into egg yolks; stir egg yolks into hot corn. Beat egg whites in bowl until stiff peaks form. Fold gently into corn mixture. Spoon ground beef mixture into four 2-ounce baking dishes. Sprinkle with olives, raisins and sliced eggs. Spoon corn mixture over top. Sprinkle with 1 tablespoon sugar. Bake at 400° F. for 15 to 18 minutes or until set. Yield: 4 servings.

ENCHILADAS — Mexico

1/2 cup oil
2/3 cup flour
1/4 cup Grandma's Spanish
   Seasoning chili powder
2 teaspoons salt
4 cups lukewarm water
11/2 pounds ground beef

2 large onions, chopped
1 small can tomato sauce
1 small can chopped olives
11/2 teaspoons salt
12 corn tortillas
1 cup (or more) shredded
   Cheddar cheese

Blend oil, flour, chili powder and 2 teaspoons salt in 2-quart saucepan. Stir in water gradually. Bring to a boil over low heat, stirring constantly. Remove from heat; set aside. Brown ground beef with onions in skillet, stirring until ground beef is crumbly; drain. Stir in tomato sauce, olives and 11/2 teaspoons salt. Spoon mixture onto tortillas. Roll tortillas to enclose filling; secure with toothpicks. Place in greased baking dish. Pour chili powder gravy over top. Sprinkle with cheese. Bake at 325° F. for 30 minutes. Yield: 12 servings.

HASH — Puerto Rico

1/4 cup chopped green pepper	1 28-ounce can tomatoes,
1/4 cup chopped onion	mashed
1/4 cup chopped mushrooms	1/4 cup seedless raisins
2 tablespoons oil	1/4 cup slivered almonds
1 pound ground round steak	1 teaspoon (about) salt
1/4 cup sliced stuffed olives	1/8 teaspoon pepper

Sauté green pepper, onion and mushrooms in oil in saucepan until onions are golden. Add ground steak. Cook over medium heat until beef is browned. Add olives, tomatoes, raisins, almonds, salt and pepper. Simmer, covered, for 20 minutes. Serve over rice. Yield: 4 servings.

MEATBALLS (ALBÓNDIGAS)— Mexico

8 ounces ground beef	2 hard-boiled eggs, chopped
8 ounces ground pork	1/2 cup raisins
1/2 cup cooked rice	2 tablespoons chopped stuffed
1 egg, beaten	olives
1/4 cup chopped onion	1 10-ounce can tomato soup
1/2 teaspoon oregano	1 soup can water
1/2 teaspoon salt	1 teaspoon chili powder
Pepper to taste	1 teaspoon dry mustard

Combine ground beef, ground pork, rice, beaten egg, onion, oregano, salt and pepper in bowl; mix well. Shape into small balls, pressing 1 small piece chopped egg, 3 raisins and 3 pieces chopped olives into center. Combine remaining ingredients in saucepan; mix well. Bring to a boil. Add meatballs. Simmer, covered, for 30 minutes. Yield: 4 to 6 servings.

MEATBALLS

1¹/2 cups soft bread crumbs
1 cup light cream
¹/2 cup chopped onion
1 tablespoon butter
12 ounces lean ground beef
8 ounces ground veal
4 ounces ground pork
1 egg
¹/4 cup chopped parsley

1¹/4 teaspoons salt
Pepper, ginger and nutmeg to
  taste
¹/4 cup butter
2 tablespoons flour
1¹/4 cups beef bouillon
¹/2 teaspoon instant coffee
  powder

Soak bread crumbs in cream in bowl for 5 minutes. Sauté onion in 1 tablespoon butter in skillet. Combine ground beef, ground veal, ground pork, bread crumbs, egg, parsley, salt, pepper and spices in bowl. Beat at medium speed for 5 minutes. Shape into 1¹/2-inch meatballs. Fry in 2 tablespoons butter in skillet. Remove meatballs; drain. Melt remaining 2 tablespoons butter in drippings in skillet. Add flour; mix well. Add bouillon and coffee powder. Cook until thickened. Add meatballs. Simmer, covered, for 30 minutes. Yield: 6 servings.

ALBÓNDIGAS — México

1¹/2 tazas de migas de pan
  suave
1 taza de crema ligera
¹/2 taza de cebolla picada
1 cucharada de mantequilla
12 onzas de carne de res
  molida
8 onzas de carne de ternera
  molida
4 onzas de carne de puerco
  molida

1 huevo
1¹/4 taza de perejil
1¹/4 cucharadita de sal
Pimienta, jengibre y nuez
  moscada al gusto
¹/4 taza de mantequilla
2 cucharadas de harina
1¹/4 tazas de caldo de res
¹/2 cucharadita de café en
  polvo

Remoje las migas de pan en la crema en una vasija durante 5 minutos. Sofría la cebolla en una cucharada de mantequilla en un sartén. Mezcle las carnes, pan, huevo, cebolla, perejil, sal, pimienta y especias en una vasija. Bata a velocidad media por 5 minutos. Dele forma de bolas de 1¹/2 pulgadas. Fría en 2 cucharadas de mantequilla en un sartén. Sáque del sartén; escurra. Ponga 2 cucharadas de mantequilla en el sartén con el residuo. Añada la harina, mezclando bien. Agregue el caldo de res y café en polvo. Cocine hasta que el jugo de carne se espese. Añada las albóndigas. Cocine lentamente por 30 minutos, tapado.

MEAT TURNOVERS — Puerto Rico

1/4 cup shortening
4 cups flour
4 teaspoons baking powder
2 teaspoons salt
1 egg, lightly beaten
1 1/4 cups water
1 1/2 pounds ground beef
1 medium onion, chopped

1 green pepper, chopped
1/2 cup chopped olives
2 hard-boiled eggs, chopped
1/2 cup raisins
1 teaspoon salt
1/2 teaspoon pepper
Oil for frying

Cut shortening into sifted flour, baking powder and 2 teaspoons salt in bowl. Add egg and water, tossing lightly to form a soft dough. Chill in refrigerator. Brown ground beef with onion and green pepper in skillet. Add remaining ingredients except oil. Simmer for 15 to 20 minutes. Roll dough to 1/16-inch thickness on floured surface. Cut into 4-inch circles. Place 1 spoonful meat sauce on each circle. Fold dough over to enclose filling; seal edges with fork. Fry in oil until golden brown. Drain on paper towels. Serve hot. Yield: 20 to 24 turnovers.

EMPANADAS DE CARNE — Puerto Rico

1/4 taza de manteca
4 tazas de harina
4 cucharaditas de polvo de
   hornear
2 cucharaditas de sal
1 huevo batido
1 1/4 tazas de agua
1 1/2 libras de carne molida
1 cebolla mediana picada

1 pimiento verde picado
1/2 taza de aceitunas picadas
2 huevos duros, picados
1/2 taza de pasas
1 cucharada de alcaparras
1 cucharadita de sal
1/2 cucharadita de pimienta
Aceite para freír

Ponga la manteca en un tazón junto con una mezcla de la harina cernida con el polvo de hornear y 2 cucharaditas de sal. Corte la manteca en pedazos muy pequeños con 2 cuchillos o un cortador especial. Mézclale 1 huevo y el agua poco a poco hasta formar una bola de masa suave. Guarde en el refrigerador. Cocine la carne, cebolla y pimiento verde en un sartén. Agregue el resto de los ingredientes salvo el aceite. Deje cocer a fuego lento por 15 a 20 minutos. Extienda la masa con un rodillo hasta que tenga 1/16 pulgada de espesor. Corte círculos de 4 pulgadas. Ponga una cucharada de la mezcla de carne en cada círculo. Doble y aplaste las orillas con la punta de un tenedor. Fríense en aceite caliente hasta que estén doradas. Escurra sobre toalla de papel. Sirva caliente.

SKILLET TACO — Mexico

8 ounces ground beef	1 21-ounce can chili con carne
1 medium onion, chopped	1 to 2 cups cooked pinto beans
1/2 clove of garlic, chopped	1/2 cup half and half
1 small green chili pepper,	Shredded lettuce
chopped	1 large package corn chips
1 21-ounce can tomatoes	1 cup shredded Cheddar cheese

Brown ground beef with onion and garlic in skillet, stirring until ground beef is crumbly; drain. Add green chili, tomatoes, chili con carne and beans. Simmer for 30 minutes. Stir in half and half. Sprinkle with shredded lettuce, corn chips and cheese. Yield: 6 to 8 servings.

BLACK BEAN STEW (FEIJOADA) — Brazil

1 pound dried black beans	8 ounces smoked sausage links
6 cups water	4 ounces chopped ham
8 ounces stew meat	1/2 cup chopped onion
1 1-pound smoked beef tongue	1 medium tomato, peeled,
1 pig's foot	chopped
3 cups water	2 tablespoons chopped parsley
1 pound spareribs, cut into	2 cloves of garlic, minced
1-rib portions	1/4 teaspoon dried chilies
8 ounces fresh pork sausage	Salt and pepper to taste
links	

Bring beans and 6 cups water to a boil in 4-quart saucepan; reduce heat. Simmer for 2 minutes; remove from heat. Let stand, covered, for 1 hour. Bring to a boil again; reduce heat. Simmer, covered, for 2 hours or until beans are nearly tender. Combine stew meat, tongue and pig's foot with 3 cups water in saucepan. Simmer, covered, for 45 minutes. Add spareribs. Simmer for 30 minutes. Add fresh sausage. Simmer for 15 minutes. Drain, reserving liquid. Cut drained meat into bite-sized pieces, discarding skin and bones. Skim reserved cooking liquid. Add to beans with chopped meat, smoked sausage, ham, onion, tomato, parsley, garlic and chilies. Simmer, covered, for 30 minutes longer. Mash beans slightly. Season to taste. Yield: 10 to 12 servings.

HAM AND MACARONI CASSEROLE

1 medium onion, chopped
1/4 cup chopped parsley
1/4 cup butter
8 ounces ground ham

6 ounces cream cheese
8 ounces macaroni, cooked,
    drained
3 ounces cream cheese

Sauté onion and parsley in butter in saucepan. Add ham and 6 ounces cream cheese. Cook until cream cheese is melted, stirring to mix well. Stir in macaroni. Spoon into greased baking dish. Chop 3 ounces cream cheese. Sprinkle over casserole. Bake at 350° F. for 15 minutes. Serve hot. Yield: 4 servings.

MACARRONES CON JAMÓN Y QUESO

1 cebolla mediana picada
1/4 taza de perejil
1/4 taza de mantequilla
8 onzas de jamón molido

6 onzas de queso crema
8 onzas de macarrones cocidos
    y colados
3 onzas de queso crema

Sofría la cebolla y el perejil en la mantequilla en un sartén. Añada el jamón y 6 onzas del queso crema. Cocínelo todo hasta que el queso esté derritido y todo esté bien mezclado. Añada los macarrones, mezclando bien. Ponga la mezcla en un molde engrasado para hornear. Corte 3 onzas de queso en cuadritos. Póngalos sobre los macarrones. Hornee a 350° F. por 15 minutos. Sirva caliente.

POSOLE

3 pounds cubed pork shoulder
6 cups water
1 small onion, chopped
1 clove of garlic, chopped

6 cups drained canned hominy
4 red chili peppers
1/2 teaspoon oregano
Salt to taste

Combine pork and water in large saucepan. Cook for 2 1/2 hours or until pork is tender. Add remaining ingredients; mix well. Simmer for 30 minutes. Serve with sopaipillas. Yield: 12 servings.

LAMB SAN GABRIEL — Mexico

2 pounds lamb shoulder
1/4 cup flour
3 tablespoons oil
1 medium onion, sliced
1 cup beef bouillon
1 1/2 cups cooked pinto beans
1   12-ounce can whole kernel
   corn, drained

1   4-ounce jar chopped
   pimento, drained
1 medium green pepper, cut
   into strips
1/2 teaspoon basil
1/2 teaspoon thyme
1 teaspoon salt
1/2 teaspoon pepper

Cut lamb into cubes. Roll in flour, coating well. Brown on all sides in hot oil in large skillet. Remove with slotted spoon. Add onion. Sauté until golden. Stir in lamb and remaining ingredients. Spoon into greased 2-quart baking dish. Bake, covered, at 350° F. for 1 hour or until lamb is tender. Yield: 6 servings.

PASTELADO — Colombia

10 pieces chicken
5 small pork chops
2 tablespoons shortening
2 cups rice
3 carrots, chopped
2 large onions, chopped
3 cloves of garlic, chopped
Oil
1   16-ounce can whole kernel
   corn, drained

1   16-ounce can green peas,
   drained
4 pimentos, chopped
24 stuffed olives
1   2-ounce bottle of capers,
   partially drained
2 teaspoons salt
1 teaspoon pepper

Brown chicken and pork in shortening in saucepan. Add enough water to cover. Simmer until meat is tender. Drain, reserving 3 cups broth. Place meats in baking dish. Cook rice in reserved broth in covered saucepan until liquid is absorbed. Sauté carrots, onions and garlic in a small amount of oil in saucepan. Add rice and remaining ingredients; mix well. Spoon over meat in baking dish. Bake, covered, at 200° F. for 1 hour or longer. Yield: 10 servings.

CHICKEN WITH RICE (ARROZ CON POLLO) — Mexico

1 medium chicken, cut up
2 tablespoons olive oil
1 cup rice
1 small onion, chopped
1 small tomato, chopped
1 green chili pepper, chopped

1 tablespoon oregano
2 cups boiling chicken broth
1 30-ounce jar stuffed olives,
   drained
1 small can peas, drained
2 tablespoons capers

Brown chicken in olive oil in saucepan. Remove chicken with slotted spoon. Add rice, onion, tomato, green chili and oregano to skillet. Sauté for several minutes. Arrange chicken over rice. Pour hot broth over chicken. Simmer, covered, for 1 hour. Add olives and water if needed for desired consistency; do not stir. Simmer until heated through. Add peas and capers at serving time. Yield: 6 servings.

CHICKEN WITH RICE (ARROZ CON POLLO) — Honduras

2 cloves of garlic
1/3 cup olive oil
2 chickens, cut up
1 large onion, chopped
1 green pepper, chopped
1 large tomato, chopped
2 tablespoons Worcestershire
   sauce
1 tablespoon catsup

Paprika, Season-All salt and
   pepper to taste
1 cup chopped pimento
1 cup sliced mushrooms
3 cups rice
2 small bottles of capers
1 small jar stuffed olives
1 cup peas

Sauté garlic in olive oil in saucepan until brown. Remove and discard garlic. Brown chicken on both sides in oil in saucepan. Remove with slotted spoon. Add onion, green pepper and tomato. Cook until onion is translucent. Stir in Worcestershire sauce, catsup, paprika, Season-All salt and pepper. Add chicken, pimento and mushrooms. Simmer, covered, until chicken is tender. Cook rice according to package instructions. Add to saucepan with capers, olives and peas. Cook until heated through. Yield: 8 servings.

CHICKEN WITH RICE — Costa Rica

1 small chicken, cut up
1 16-ounce can peas
1 onion, chopped
1 small can mushrooms
2 large stalks celery, chopped
4 medium carrots, sliced

2 large tomatoes, chopped
1 jar olives, chopped
1 8-ounce can tomato paste
Garlic, salt and pepper to taste
1 large green pepper, chopped
1 package long grain rice

Cook chicken in water to cover in saucepan. Drain, reserving broth. Cool chicken. Shred, discarding bones. Combine undrained peas, onion, mushrooms, celery, carrots, tomatoes, olives, tomato paste and green pepper in large saucepan. Add enough water to cover. Season with garlic, salt and pepper to taste. Add chicken. Bring to a boil; reduce heat. Simmer until carrots are tender. Prepare rice according to package directions, substituting reserved broth for water. Serve chicken mixture over rice. Yield: 12 servings.

ARROZ CON POLLO — Costa Rica

1 pollo pequeño, en pedazos
1 lata de guisantes, tamaño
    mediano
1 cebolla, picada
1 lata pequeña de hongas
2 tallos de apio picados
4 zanahorias picados

2 tomates grandes picados
1 lata de aceitunas picadas
1 lata de 8 onzas de puré
    concentrado de tomates
1 pimiento verde picado
Sal, pimienta y ajo
1 paquete de arroz, grano largo

Hierva el pollo en agua en una olla. Cuele. Guarde el caldo. Enfríe el pollo. Desmenuce el pollo. Combine los guisantes con su líquido, cebolla, hongos, apio, zanahorias, tomates, aceitunas, puré concentrado de tomate y pimiento verde. Asegúrese que el líquido cubre los ingredientes; a no ser así, ponga más agua. Añada sal, pimiento y ajo al gusto. Ponga el pollo en esta mezcla. Caliente hasta hervir; después deje cocinar a fuego lento hasta que las zanahorias se pongan blandas. Siga las instrucciones en el paquete para preparar el arroz, pero use el caldo de pollo en vez de agua. Sirva el pollo encima del arroz.

CHICKEN WITH RICE — Puerto Rico

2 ounces chopped bacon
4 ounces chopped ham
2 cloves of garlic, minced
2 tomatoes, chopped
1 green pepper, chopped
1 medium onion, chopped
1/2 teaspoon pepper
1 tablespoon salt
1/2 teaspoon oregano

1/4 cup anise-flavored oil
1 1/2 pounds chicken pieces
3 cups rice
1/2 cup chopped olives
1 tablespoon capers
3 cups water
4 pimentos, cut into strips
1 cup cooked peas

Sauté first 9 ingredients in oil in saucepan. Add chicken. Simmer, covered, for 30 to 40 minutes or until chicken is almost tender. Add rice, olives, capers and water. Bring to a boil. Cook until mixture begins to cook dry. Reduce heat. Simmer, covered, for 15 to 20 minutes or until rice is tender. Add enough additional water to make rice tender if necessary. Fluff with fork. Spoon into serving dish. Garnish with pimentos and peas. Yield: 6 to 8 servings. Prepare oil with aniseed flavor by sautéing 1/2 cup aniseed in oil in skillet until oil is color of seed. Discard seed. Yield: 6 servings.

ARROZ CON POLLO — Puerto Rico

2 onzas de tocino picado
4 onzas de jamón picado
2 dientes de ajo, picado fino
2 tomates picados
1 pimiento verde, picado
1 cebolla mediana picada
1/2 cucharadita de pimienta
1 cucharada de sal
1/2 cucharadita de orégano

1/4 taza de aceite con achiote
2 1/2 libras de pollo partido
3 tazas de arroz
1/2 taza de aceitunas picadas
1 cucharada de alcaparras
3 tazas de agua
4 pimientos rojos en rajas
1 taza de guisantes cocidos

Sofría los 9 primeros ingredientes en aceite en una olla grande. Añada el pollo. Cocine por 30 a 40 minutos tapado. Agregue el arroz, las aceitunas, alcaparras y agua. Deje hervir destapado hasta que empiece a secarse. Baje el fuego y tape. Cueza por 15 a 20 minutos hasta que el arroz esté suave. Revuelva un poquito con un tenedor. Sirva en un platón grande adornado con rajas de pimiento rojo y guisantes. Para preparar el aceite con achiote, fría 1/2 taza de achiote en aceite en un sartén hasta que suelte su color. Descarte el achiote.

CHICKEN ENCHILADAS

5 chicken breasts
1 medium onion, chopped
8 ounces cream cheese,
  softened
1 cup milk
1 can cream of chicken soup
1 8-ounce can salsa

24 corn tortillas
Oil
8 ounces Cheddar cheese,
  shredded
Chopped olives
Chopped green onions

Cook chicken in water to cover in saucepan; drain. Chop chicken. Combine with onion and cream cheese in bowl. Mix milk, soup and salsa in small bowl. Cook tortillas in a small amount of oil in skillet. Place chicken mixture on tortillas. Roll tortillas to enclose filling. Place in 9 x 13-inch baking pan. Pour soup mixture over top. Sprinkle with Cheddar cheese, olives and green onions. Bake, covered, at 350° F. for 30 minutes. Bake, uncovered, for 10 minutes longer. Yield: 24 enchiladas.

ENCHILADAS DE POLLO

5 pechugas de pollo grandes
1 cebolla mediana picada
8 onzas de queso crema,
  suavizado
1 taza de leche
1 lata sopa de crema de pollo
1 lata de 8 onzas de salsa

24 tortillas de maíz
Aceite
8 onzas de queso de Cheddar
  rallado
Aceitunas picadas
Cebollas verdes picadas

Hierva el pollo en agua en una olla. Corte en pedazos. Mezcle con cebolla y queso crema en una vasija. Mezcle la leche, la sopa y la salsa en una otra vasija. Caliente las tortillas en un poco de aceite en un sartén. Ponga la mezcla de pollo en las tortillas. Enrolle las tortillas y póngalas en una cacerola de 9 por 13 pulgadas. Cubra con la mezcla de la sopa. Ponga encima el queso de Cheddar, las acieitunas y las cebollas verdes. Hornee tapado a 350° F. por 30 minutos. Hornee por 10 minutos destapado.

GREEN CHICKEN ENCHILADAS

2 chickens
1 16-ounce can tomatoes
2 to 3 4-ounce cans green
   chilies
Salt, onion salt and garlic salt
   to taste
2 to 3 cans evaporated milk

2 to 3 cans cream of
   mushroom soup
Oil for frying
24 corn tortillas
1 pound American cheese,
   shredded
1 can mushrooms

Cook chickens in water to cover in large saucepan until tender; drain. Chop chicken into bite-sized pieces. Place tomatoes in bowl; chop with side of spoon. Add green chilies and seasonings; mix well. Combine evaporated milk and soup in bowl; mix until smooth. Heat oil in skillet. Fry tortillas 1 at a time in oil. Alternate layers of tortillas, chicken, tomato mixture, soup mixture and cheese in 9 x 13-inch baking dish until all ingredients are used. Top with mushrooms. Bake at 350° F. until bubbly. Yield: 8 to 10 servings.

CHICKEN AND JALAPEÑO CASSEROLE

1 package corn chips
2 cups chopped cooked chicken
2 cans cream of chicken soup
2 small cans evaporated milk

1 onion, chopped
2 (or more) jalapeño peppers,
   chopped
Shredded cheese

Layer corn chips and chicken in baking dish. Combine soup, evaporated milk, onion and peppers in saucepan. Heat to the boiling point, stirring to mix well. Pour over chicken. Bake at 250° F. for 30 minutes. Top with cheese. Bake just until cheese is melted. Yield: 6 servings.

ROASTED CHICKEN BREASTS WITH CHILIES
(PECHUGA ASADA CON RAJAS) — Mexico

4 chicken breast filets
1/2 teaspoon salt
4 to 10 strips canned jalapeño
   peppers

1 tomato, chopped
1 medium onion, sliced
Oil

Slice chicken into narrow strips. Season with salt. Grill to desired degree of doneness on grill. Sauté jalapeño peppers, tomato and onion in oil in skillet; drain. Place chicken on serving platter. Top with vegetables. Serve with warm tortillas. Yield: 2 to 4 servings.

SAVORY CHICKEN PIE (EMPANADA)

2 tablespoons shortening
2 tablespoons butter
3 cups flour

1/2 teaspoon salt
3/4 cup milk
4 egg yolks, lightly beaten

Cut shortening and butter into mixture of flour and salt in bowl until crumbly. Stir in milk and egg yolks; shape into ball. Let rest, covered, for 1 hour. Divide into 2 portions. Roll 1 portion thin on floured surface. Fit into 10-inch pie plate. Fill with Chicken Filling. Top with remaining pastry. Brush with a small amount of additional milk. Bake at 375° F. for 45 minutes or until golden brown; cover edge with foil if necessary to prevent overbrowning. Yield: 6 servings.

Chicken Filling

3 chicken breasts, about
   2 1/2 pounds
2 tablespoons butter
1 1/2 teaspoons salt
1/8 teaspoon pepper
1/4 cup chopped onion
2 tablespoons parsley

1/4 cup tomato sauce
1 tablespoon vinegar
Milk
3 tablespoons cornstarch
1/2 cup finely chopped onion
1/4 cup chopped parsley

Brown chicken in butter in skillet. Sprinkle with salt and pepper. Add 1/4 cup onion, 2 tablespoons parsley, tomato sauce and vinegar. Simmer, covered, for 20 minutes or until chicken is tender. Cool. Drain, reserving broth. Cut chicken into bite-sized pieces. Skim and strain broth. Combine with enough milk to measure 2 1/2 cups liquid. Blend broth mixture with cornstarch in large saucepan. Cook until thickened. Stir a small amount of hot mixture into egg yolks; stir egg yolks into hot mixture. Stir in remaining onion, parsley and chicken.

CHICKEN IN PEANUT SAUCE
(GALINHA CON MÔLHO DE AMENDOIM) — Brazil

1 onion, chopped
1/2 cup chopped green pepper
3 tablespoons butter
1 chicken, cut up
Garlic powder
11/2 cups chicken broth

1/2 teaspoon coriander
1/2 teaspoon ginger
Salt and pepper to taste
1/2 cup very finely chopped
    peanuts

Sauté onion and green pepper in butter in skillet. Sprinkle chicken with garlic powder. Add to skillet. Cook until brown on both sides. Add broth, seasonings and peanuts. Simmer, covered, until chicken is tender enough to fall away from bones. Remove chicken with slotted spoon. Discard bones and skin. Return chicken to sauce. Serve with rice and fried bananas. Garnish with black olives. May substitute peanut butter for peanuts. Yield: 4 servings.

CHICKEN IN VINEGAR
(POLLO EN VINAGRE) — Venezuela

1 3-pound chicken, cut up
1/2 cup flour
1 teaspoon salt
1/4 cup oil
1 4-ounce can mushrooms
1 can artichoke hearts
2 tomatoes, peeled, chopped
1 green pepper, cut into strips
4 cloves of garlic, crushed

2 tablespoons oil
2 tablespoons vinegar
1 bay leaf
Juice of 1 lemon
1 tablespoon chopped parsley
1/2 cup red wine
1/2 teaspoon salt
Pepper to taste

Roll chicken in mixture of flour and 1 teaspoon salt, coating well. Brown in 1/4 cup oil in saucepan. Drain mushrooms and artichoke hearts, reserving liquid. Add enough water to reserved juices to measure 1 cup. Add liquid, tomatoes, green pepper, garlic, 2 tablespoons oil, vinegar and bay leaf to chicken. Simmer for 10 minutes. Add lemon juice, parsley, wine, 1/2 teaspoon salt and pepper. Simmer for 20 minutes or until chicken is tender. Stir in mushrooms and artichoke hearts. Heat to serving temperature. Remove bay leaf. Serve with rice. Yield: 4 servings.

RED SNAPPER WITH GREEN CHILIES
(HUACHINANGO EN CHILE VERDE)

2 small jalapeño peppers, seeded, chopped	Oil
1 medium onion, chopped	1 red snapper
2 cloves of garlic, minced	2 tomatoes, finely chopped
	1/4 teaspoon salt

Sauté chilies, onion and garlic in a small amount of oil in skillet until tender. Add fish. Cook until browned on both sides. Add tomatoes and salt; reduce heat. Cook over medium-low heat for 20 minutes or until fish flakes easily.

PICKLED FISH (SEVICHE) — Mexico

1 pound red snapper fillets	1/3 cup water
1/3 cup white wine	2 tablespoons vinegar
1/3 cup lime juice	1/2 teaspoon salt
1 medium onion, thinly sliced	1/4 teaspoon crushed dried
1/4 teaspoon salt	chilies

Cut fish into 1/2-inch strips. Combine with boiling water to cover in bowl; drain immediately. Combine fish, wine and lime juice in bowl. Marinate in refrigerator for 3 hours. Mix onion, 1/4 teaspoon salt and 1/3 cup water in bowl. Let stand for 20 minutes. Rinse and drain onion. Combine onion, vinegar, 1/2 teaspoon salt and chilies with fish. Chill, covered, for 2 to 3 hours. Yield: 6 to 8 servings.

SHRIMP CURRY — Costa Rica

2 large onions, chopped	1 tablespoon shredded coconut
2 cloves of garlic, minced	3/4 tablespoon flour
3 tablespoons butter	1 1/2 teaspoons sugar
1 1/2 cups water	3/4 teaspoon curry powder
2 tomatoes, peeled, chopped	1/4 teaspoon ginger
1 large apple, chopped	Salt and pepper to taste
1/2 cup chopped celery	1 1/2 pounds peeled shrimp

Sauté onions and garlic in butter in saucepan until lightly browned. Stir in water. Bring to a boil. Add tomatoes, apple, celery and coconut. Blend flour, sugar and seasonings with enough cold water to make a smooth paste. Stir into simmering mixture. Simmer for 30 to 40 minutes or until vegetables are tender, stirring occasionally. Stir in shrimp. Cook for 5 minutes. Serve on rice. Yield: 6 servings.

SHRIMP WITH EGGS (FRITADA DE CAMARAO)

1 cup chopped onion	4 teaspoons cornstarch
1/2 cup chopped parsley	1/2 teaspoon salt
2 tablespoons butter	1/8 teaspoon cayenne pepper
1 pound peeled shrimp	4 eggs, separated
1 cup chopped peeled tomatoes	1/4 teaspoon salt
1/4 cup coconut milk or milk	1 small onion, sliced into rings

Sauté 1 cup onion and parsley in butter in saucepan just until tender. Add shrimp and tomatoes. Cook, covered, for 10 minutes. Blend coconut milk, cornstarch, 1/2 teaspoon salt and cayenne pepper in cup. Stir into shrimp mixture. Cook until thickened, stirring constantly. Keep warm. Beat egg whites and 1/4 teaspoon salt in bowl until stiff peaks form. Beat egg yolks in bowl for 5 minutes. Fold into egg whites. Spoon shrimp mixture into 8 x 8-inch baking dish. Mound egg mixture over top. Sprinkle with onion rings. Bake at 375° F. for 20 to 25 minutes or until set. Serve immediately. Yield: 4 servings.

GREEN CHILIES CASSEROLE — Mexico

12 corn tortillas	1 onion, chopped
1 cup shredded Cheddar cheese	1 10-ounce can bouillon
1 5-ounce can chopped green	1 can cream of mushroom soup
chilies	1 can cream of chicken soup

Cut each tortilla into 6 pieces. Alternate layers of cheese, green chilies, onion and tortillas in 2-quart casserole until all ingredients are used, ending with cheese. Combine bouillon and soups in bowl; mix well. Pour over layers. Bake at 350° F. for 35 to 40 minutes. Yield: 6 servings.

CHEESY PEPPER SOUFFLÉ — Mexico

2 green peppers, chopped	4 cups shredded Monterey
4 hot peppers, chopped	Jack cheese
1 tablespoon oil	10 eggs, beaten
2 cups cottage cheese	1 cup milk

Sauté peppers in oil in skillet for 3 minutes. Combine with cottage cheese and Monterey Jack cheese in bowl; mix well. Spread in 9 x 13-inch baking dish. Combine eggs and milk in bowl; mix well. Pour over cheese mixture. Bake at 350° F. for 35 to 40 minutes or until light brown. Yield: 8 servings.

REFRIED BEANS — Mexico

1 pound dried pinto beans
8 ounces salt pork, chopped
1 tablespoon chili powder
1 clove of garlic, chopped

1 teaspoon salt
2 tablespoons shortening
1 medium onion, thinly sliced

Soak beans in water to cover in bowl overnight. Drain. Add boiling water to cover and salt pork. Simmer for 2 hours or until tender. Stir in chili powder, garlic and salt. Melt shortening in large skillet. Add beans 1 spoonful at a time, mashing well. Cook over low heat for 15 minutes, stirring occasionally. Spoon into serving bowl. Top with cheese and onion. Yield: 8 servings.

GREEN BEANS — Mexico

1 pound green beans
1 clove of garlic, minced
1/4 cup chopped green pepper
1 cup onion rings
1 tablespoon oil

1 16-ounce can tomatoes
1/4 cup chopped green chilies
1/4 teaspoon oregano
1 teaspoon salt
1/8 teaspoon pepper

Break green beans into bite-sized pieces. Cook in water to cover in saucepan just until tender; drain. Sauté garlic, green pepper and onion in oil in skillet. Add tomatoes, chilies, oregano, salt and pepper; mix well. Simmer for 15 minutes. Spoon beans onto serving plate. Spoon tomato mixture over top.
Yield: 4 servings.

GREEN CORN (ELOTE) — Mexico

8 ears of young corn
3 tablespoons butter
1 cup milk
2 tablespoons chopped green
   pepper

1 egg, beaten
2 tablespoons chopped
   pimentos
1 tablespoon sugar
1 teaspoon salt

Cut kernels from corn. Scrape pulp from cobs. Mix with corn in bowl. Heat butter in skillet. Add corn. Sauté until golden. Stir in remaining ingredients. Simmer until thickened. Yield: 8 servings.

POTATO AND JALAPEÑO CASSEROLE — Mexico

8 large potatoes
3 large onions
Oil for frying
6 jalpeño peppers, thinly sliced

1 pound Monterey Jack
   cheese, shredded
Salt and pepper to taste

Peel and slice potatoes and onions. Fry potatoes in oil in skillet just until tender; drain. Alternate layers of potatoes, onions, jalapeños, cheese, salt and pepper in 9 x 13-inch baking dish. Bake at 300° F. for 30 minutes. Yield: 10 servings.

PAPAS CON JALAPEÑOS — México

8 papas grandes
3 cebollas grandes
6 jalapeños en rebanadas
Aceite para freír

1/2 kilogramo de queso tipo
   Monterey, rallado
Sal y pimienta

Pele las papas y las cebollas y corte en rebanadas. Fría las papas en aceite sin dorar en un sartén. Escurra. Pónganse en una cacerola de 9 por 11 pulgadas, capas sucesivas de papas, cebollas, jalapeños y queso con sal y pimiento al gusto. Hornee a 300° F. por 30 minutos.

STUFFED POTATOES (PAPAS RELLENAS)

8 ounces ground beef
1 medium onion, chopped
1 hard-boiled egg, chopped
2 tablespoons chopped raisins
2 tablespoons chopped black
   olives
1/4 teaspoon oregano

1/8 teaspoon cayenne pepper
1/2 teaspoon salt
1/4 teaspoon pepper
3 cups chilled mashed potatoes
1 egg yolk, beaten
1/2 cup flour
Oil for deep frying

Brown ground beef with onion in skillet, stirring until ground beef is crumbly; drain. Stir in hard-boiled egg, raisins, olives, oregano, cayenne pepper, salt and pepper. Blend potatoes, egg yolk and flour in bowl. Pat 1/4 cup at a time to 4-inch circle on lightly floured waxed paper. Place about 2 tablespoons ground beef mixture on each circle. Roll up potato to enclose filling, lifting waxed paper to help shape into 4-inch log. Deep-fry in 360° oil for 3 minutes or until golden; drain. Serve hot. Yield: 12 servings.

SQUASH CASSEROLE

1 1/2 pounds squash, chopped
1 onion, chopped
2 tablespoons butter
1 4-ounce can chopped green
    chilies, drained
2 tablespoons flour

Salt and pepper to taste
1 1/2 cups shredded Monterey
    Jack cheese
1 egg, beaten
1 cup cottage cheese

Sauté squash and onion in butter in skillet. Stir in chilies, flour and seasonings. Pour into greased 2-quart baking dish. Sprinkle with cheese. Combine remaining ingredients in bowl; mix well. Pour over casserole. Bake at 400° F. for 45 to 50 minutes. Yield: 8 servings.

SQUASH WITH PEPPERS — Mexico

1 medium onion, chopped
2 tablespoons oil
1 1/2 pounds yellow squash,
    chopped

1 1/2 cups chopped tomatoes
2 cloves of garlic, minced
Salt and pepper to taste
2 or 3 hot peppers

Sauté onion in oil in saucepan. Add squash, tomatoes, garlic, salt, pepper and a small amount of water. Simmer until tender-crisp. Add hot peppers. Simmer until tender. Yield: 4 servings.

SPINACH CHALUPAS CASSEROLE
(CHALUPAS DE ESPINACAS) — Mexico

2 pounds spinach
1/2 cup minced onion
2 cloves of garlic, minced
Tabasco sauce to taste
Salt to taste
1/2 cup cracker crumbs

1 egg, beaten
18 flour tortillas
1 1/2 cups cream
1 1/2 cups shredded Cheddar
    cheese

Combine spinach with a small amount of water in saucepan. Cook just until tender; drain well. Chop spinach. Combine with onion, garlic, Tabasco sauce and salt in bowl; mix well. Stir in cracker crumbs and egg. Spoon mixture onto tortillas; roll to enclose filling. Place in baking dish. Pour cream over rolls. Let stand for 4 to 5 hours. Sprinkle with cheese. Bake at 300° F. for 45 minutes or until golden brown. Yield: 9 servings.

PUMPKIN SOUFFLÉ (SOUFFLÉ DE ABÓBORA) — Brazil

1¹/₂ 16-ounce cans pumpkin
1 tablespoon butter, softened
1 tablespoon cream
3 eggs, separated
1 teaspoon salt

Combine pumpkin, butter, cream, beaten egg yolks and salt in bowl; mix well. Beat egg whites in bowl until stiff peaks form. Fold gently into pumpkin mixture. Spoon into buttered baking dish. Bake at 375° F. until set and golden. Yield: 6 servings.

CANDIED SWEET POTATOES — Peru

Sweet potatoes
Cloves
Cinnamon stick
Brown sugar
Cinnamon

Peel sweet potatoes and cut into thin strips. Combine with water to cover, cloves and stick of cinnamon in saucepan. Cook until tender. Add brown sugar to taste. Place in serving dish. Remove cloves and cinnamon stick. Sprinkle with ground cinnamon to taste.

CAMOTE CON DULCE — Perú

Camotes
Clavos de olor
Canela en raja
Azúcar moreno
Canela en polvo

Pele los camotes y corte en rajitas. Ponga en un olla con agua, clavos de olor y una raja de canela. Cocine hasta suavizarse. Añada azúcar moreno al gusto y déjese espesar. Póngalo en una dulcera y rociar con canela en polvo.

VEGETABLE FRITA

1/2 small onion, chopped
1/3 cup oil
3 to 4 green peppers, chopped
2 eggplant, peeled, chopped
1 cup wine
4 tomatoes, peeled, chopped
Oil

1 beef bouillon cube
Parsley, oregano, basil, garlic
  salt, salt and pepper to taste
4 zucchini, chopped
1 cup sliced mushrooms
  (optional)

Sauté onion in 1/3 cup oil in saucepan. Add green peppers. Sauté until tender. Add eggplant. Cook over low heat for 15 minutes, stirring frequently. Stir in wine. Cook for 10 to 15 minutes or until eggplant is tender. Sauté tomatoes in a small amount of oil in small saucepan. Add bouillon cube and seasonings; mix well. Add to eggplant mixture. Stir in zucchini. Cook until zucchini is tender and mixture has thickened to desired consistency. Stir in mushrooms. Yield: 8 servings.

SPANISH-STYLE RICE — Mexico

1 cup rice
1 onion, chopped
2 tablespoons oil
1 green pepper, chopped

1 cup chopped tomatoes
2 teaspoons chili powder
1 teaspoon salt
1 cup boiling water

Sauté rice and onion in oil in saucepan. Stir in remaining ingredients. Bring to a boil; reduce heat. Simmer, covered, for 30 minutes or until rice is tender. Yield: 4 servings.

BARBECUE SAUCE — Venezuela

1 avocado, chopped
2 tomatoes, peeled, chopped
1 cup olive oil
3 tablespoons vinegar
2 onions, finally chopped

1 tablespoon chopped parsley
1 teaspoon prepared mustard
1 red pepper, seeded, chopped
1/2 teaspoon salt

Combine avocado and tomatoes in bowl. Mash with fork until well mixed. Mix remaining ingredients in small bowl. Add to avocado mixture; mix well. Use as barbecue sauce. Yield: 4 cups.

SAVORY SAUCE — El Salvador

1 large green pepper
1 medium onion
6 medium tomatoes

1 15-ounce can tomato sauce
1/2 teaspoon garlic salt
1/2 teaspoon cumin

Chop pepper and onion. Peel and chop tomatoes. Combine all ingredients in saucepan; mix well. Simmer for 30 minutes. Use with meats or as sauce for vegetables. Yield: 4 to 6 servings.

SALSA SABROSA — El Salvador

1 pimiento verde grande
1 cebolla mediana
6 tomates medianos
1 lata de 15 onzas de salsa de
  tomate

1/2 cucharadita de sal de ajo
1/2 cucharadita de comino en
  polvo

Corte en pedacitos el pimiento y la cebolla. Ponga en un sartén. Pele y corte en pedacitos los tomates. Ponga los tomates, la salsa de tomtate, el sal de ajo y el comino en polvo en el sartén; mezcle bien. Cocine durante 30 minutos. Se puede usar con cualquier carne o como una salsa sabrosa sobre vegetales.

YEAST BREAD — Chile

1 package dry yeast
1/2 cup lukewarm water
1/2 cup butter, softened
1/2 cup sugar

2 teaspoons salt
2 eggs, beaten
1 1/2 cups lukewarm water
6 cups flour

Dissolve yeast in 1/2 cup water. Cream butter, sugar and salt in mixer bowl until light and fluffy. Blend in eggs. Add 1 1/2 cups water. Beat until smooth. Add yeast mixture and flour; mix well. Let stand at room temperature for 45 minutes. Spoon into 2 greased and floured loaf pans. Let rise, covered, in warm place until doubled in bulk. Bake at 350° F. for 45 minutes. Yield: 2 loaves.

BREAD RING

Peel of 1 lemon, chopped
Peel of 1 orange, chopped
1/4 cup aniseed
2 cups oil
6 packages yeast
4 cups warm water

Salt
4 eggs, beaten
2 cups sugar
5 pounds (about) flour
Almonds

Sauté fruit peels in skillet until light brown. Cool. Mix aniseed with oil in bowl. Dissolve yeast in warm water in large bowl. Add salt, eggs, sugar, oil mixture and flour; mix well. Add fruit peel. Knead on floured surface until elastic. Place in greased bowl, turning to grease surface. Let rise until doubled in bulk. Shape into ring on baking sheet. Sprinkle with almonds and additional sugar. Bake at 350° F. for 30 to 40 minutes or until brown. Yield: 1 loaf.

ROSCA

Cáscara de 1 limón, picada
Cáscara de 1 naranja, picada
1/4 taza de semilla de anís
2 tazas de aceite
6 onzas de levadura activa
4 tazas de agua tibia

Sal
4 huevos batidos
2 tazas de azúcar
5 libras de harina
Almendras

Sofría las cáscaras de limón y naranja en un sartén hasta que estén doradas. Enfríe. Mezcle las semillas de anís con el aceite en una vasija. Disuelva la levadura en agua tibia en una vasija grande. Añada la sal, los huevos, el azúcar, aceite y harina; mezcle bien. Añada las cáscaras. Amase sobre una superficie enharinada hasta tener una masa elástica. Ponga la masa en una vasija engrasada y voltéela de modo que quede completamente engrasada por fuera. Deje reposar para subir hasta doblarse. Moldee la masa en forma de rosca sobre un molde de hornear. Ponga almendras y más azúcar encima. Hornee a 350° F. por 30 a 40 minutos o hasta que se dore.

BISCUITS WITH CHILIES

1 tablespoon sesame seed	1/2 teaspoon soda
1 tablespoon dry yeast	1 teaspoon salt
Pinch of sugar	3/4 cup buttermilk
2 tablespoons warm water	1/4 cup chopped roasted red
2 tablespoons butter	and green chilies
1 1/2 cups unbleached flour	2 tablespoons melted butter
1/2 cup white cornmeal	1 teaspoon sesame seed
1 1/2 teaspoons baking powder	

Sprinkle 1 tablespoon sesame seed into buttered 10-inch baking pan. Dissolve yeast and sugar in warm water. Cut 2 tablespoons butter into mixture of dry ingredients in bowl. Add buttermilk, yeast and chilies. Knead several strokes on floured surface. Shape into 1 1/4-inch balls. Place in prepared pan. Let rise, covered, in warm place for 40 minutes or until doubled in bulk. Drizzle with melted butter. Sprinkle with 1 teaspoon sesame seed. Bake at 425° F. for 20 minutes or until golden brown. Yield: 16 biscuits.

JALAPEÑO CORN BREAD

3 cups cornmeal	1 1/2 cups shredded longhorn
2 1/2 cups milk	cheese
1/2 cup oil	1/2 cup chopped jalapeño
3 eggs, beaten	peppers
1 large onion, chopped	Crumbled crisp-fried bacon
1 cup canned cream-style corn	Chopped red pepper

Combine all ingredients in mixer bowl; mix well. Pour into greased 9 x 13-inch baking pan. Bake at 400° F. for 45 minutes or until brown. Yield: 10 servings.

CHURROS

3 1/2 cups flour	2 eggs
1 tablespoon baking powder	1/2 teaspoon vanilla extract
1 teaspoon salt	Oil for deep frying
2 cups milk, scalded, cooled	

Combine dry ingredients in bowl. Add milk, eggs and vanilla; mix well. Spoon into pastry bag fitted with large tip. Press in strips into 400° oil in saucepan. Deep-fry until brown; drain. Garnish with confectioners' sugar or cinnamon-sugar. Yield: 8 servings.

SOPAIPILLAS

1 package dry yeast
1/4 cup warm water
4 cups sifted flour
1 teaspoon baking powder
1 teaspoon sugar

1 1/2 teaspoons salt
1 tablespoon shortening
1 1/4 cups milk, scalded, cooled
Oil for deep frying

Dissolve yeast in warm water in cup. Combine dry ingredients in bowl. Cut in shortening until crumbly. Add yeast and milk; mix well. Knead 15 to 20 times on floured surface. Let stand for 10 minutes. Roll 1/4 inch thick. Cut as desired. Deep-fry in hot oil until crisp. Yield: 2 dozen.

BANANA-NUT CAKE — Colombia

2/3 cup shortening
2 1/2 cups sifted flour
1 2/3 cups sugar
1 1/4 teaspoons baking powder
1 teaspoon soda
1 teaspoon salt
1 1/4 cups mashed bananas

1/3 cup buttermilk
2/3 cup chopped walnuts
1/2 cup melted butter
1 cup packed brown sugar
1/4 cup hot milk
3 1/4 cups (about)
    confectioners' sugar

Cream shortening in mixer bowl until light and fluffy. Add sifted flour, sugar, baking powder, soda and salt. Add bananas and buttermilk; mix well. Stir in walnuts. Pour into 2 baking parchment-lined 9-inch cake pans. Bake at 350° F. for 35 minutes. Cool in pans for 10 minutes. Remove to wire rack to cool completely. Blend butter and brown sugar in saucepan. Bring to a boil. Cook for 1 minute or until slightly thickened, stirring constantly. Cool for 15 minutes. Beat in hot milk. Add confectioners' sugar, beating until of spreading consistency. Spread between layers and over top and side of cake. Yield: 12 servings.

FIESTA BANANA CAKE — Mexico

1/2 cup butter, softened	3/4 teaspoon salt
1 1/3 cups sugar	1/2 cup sour milk
2 eggs	1 teaspoon baking powder
1 teaspoon vanilla extract	1 teaspoon soda
1 cup mashed bananas	3 cups whipped cream
2 cups sifted flour	Cherries

Cream butter and sugar in mixer bowl until light. Blend in eggs, vanilla and bananas. Add flour and salt alternately with sour milk, mixing well after each addition. Stir in baking powder and soda. Pour into greased and floured 9 x 13-inch cake pan. Bake at 375° F. for 25 minutes. Cool completely. Frost with whipped cream. Garnish with cherries arranged as flower petals. Store in refrigerator. Yield: 8 to 12 servings.

PASTEL DE PLÁTANOS PARA UNA FIESTA — México

1/2 taza de mantequilla, suavizada	1/2 taza de leche agria
1 1/3 tazas de azúcar	1 cucharadita de polvo de hornear
2 huevos	1 cucharadita de bicarbonato de soda
1 cucharadita de vainilla	3 tazas de crema batida
1 taza de plátano majado	Cerezas
2 tazas de harina cernida	
3/4 cucharadita de sal	

Bata la mantequilla y azúcar en una vasija hasta quedar cremoso. Añada los huevos, la vainilla y el plátano; bata bien. Añada la harina y sal alternando con la leche agria, mezclando bien después de cada adición. Añada el polvo de hornear y bicarbonato de soda. Ponga en un molde de 9 por 13 pulgadas, engrasado y enharinado. Hornee a 375° F. por 25 minutos. Deje enfriar completemente. Ponga la crema batida encima del pastel. Adorne con tajadas de cerezas arregladas como pétalos de flores. Guárdese en el refrigerador.

CHRISTMAS CAKES

3 cups seedless raisins
4¹/₂ cups dried fruit
2 cups rum
2¹/₂ cups butter, softened
1¹/₂ cups sugar
1¹/₂ cups packed brown sugar
12 egg yolks

4¹/₂ cups flour
2 tablespoons baking powder
1 tablespoon baking cocoa
1 tablespoon cloves
1 tablespoon cinnamon
12 egg whites, stiffly beaten

Soak raisins and dried fruit in rum in bowl. Cream butter in mixer bowl until light. Add sugars gradually, beating constantly. Blend in egg yolks 1 at a time. Drain fruit, reserving rum. Mix fruit with ¹/₂ cup flour. Sift remaining flour with baking powder, cocoa and spices. Add to sugar mixture alternately with rum. Fold in stiffly beaten egg whites and fruit. Pour into 4 greased and floured 8-inch cake pans. Bake at 350° F. for 35 to 40 minutes. Remove to wire rack. Garnish with confectioners' sugar and additional dried fruit while warm. Yield: 4 cakes.

TORTAS NEGRAS DE PASCUA

¹/₂ kilogramo de pasas sin
   semillas
2 tazas de ron
600 gramos de mantequilla
   suavizada
¹/₄ kilogramo de azúcar
¹/₄ kilogramo de azúcar
   moreno muy compacto

12 yemas de huevo
³/₄ kilogramo de harina
2 cucharadas de polve de
   hornear
1 cucharada de polvo de cacao
1 cucharada de clavo en polvo
1 cucharada de canela en polvo
12 claras de huevo

Remoje las pasas y las frutas secas en el ron. Bata la mantequilla en un tazón grande. Añada los azúcares poco a poco sin dejar de batir. Añada las yemas una por una. Escurra las frutas reservando el ron. Mezcle las frutas con ¹/₂ taza de harina. Cierna la harina que queda con el polvo de hornear, el cacao y las especias. Añada a la mezcla del azúcar alternando con el ron. Agregue las claras batidas a punto de nieve y las frutas. Vacíese en 4 moldes engrasados y enharindos de 8 pulgadas. Hornee a 350° F. por 35 a 40 ninutos. Cubra con azúcar en polvo y más frutas secas mientras esté todavía un poco caliente.

PIÑA COLADA CAKE — Mexico

1 18-ounce package yellow
cake mix
1 small package vanilla instant
pudding mix
1/2 cup piña colada mix
1/2 cup rum

1/3 cup oil
4 eggs
1 cup sifted confectioners'
sugar
1 to 2 tablespoons piña colada
mix

Combine cake mix, pudding mix, 1/2 cup piña colada mix, rum, oil and eggs in bowl; mix well. Pour into greased 10-inch bundt or tube pan. Bake at 350° F. for 50 to 55 minutes. Remove to wire rack to cool slightly. Blend confectioners' sugar and 1 to 2 tablespoons piña colada mix in bowl. Drizzle over cake. Yield: 16 servings.

BRIGADEIROS — Brazil

1 14-ounce can sweetened
condensed milk
2 tablespoons baking cocoa

2 tablespoons margarine,
softened
Chocolate sprinkles

Combine condensed milk, cocoa and margarine in saucepan; mix well. Cook over low heat until mixture pulls away from side of pan, stirring constantly. Spread on buttered plate; cool. Shape into small balls with buttered hands. Roll in chocolate sprinkles. Yield: 1 pound.

BURNT MILK CANDY (LECHE QUEMADA) — Mexico

2 cups milk
2 1/4 cups sugar

1/2 teaspoon cinnamon
1 cup chopped pecans

Bring milk, sugar and cinnamon to a boil in saucepan over low heat. Cook until mixture thickens and leaves side of pan, stirring frequently. Cool slightly. Stir in pecans. Beat until mixture thickens. Drop by spoonfuls onto waxed paper. Let stand until firm. Yield: 2 pounds.

PRALINES (PLANQUETAS) — Mexico

1 cup sugar	1/4 cup butter
1 cup packed brown sugar	1 teaspoon vinegar
1 cup water	1 pound pecans, broken

Combine sugars, water and butter in saucepan. Bring to a boil over medium heat, stirring until sugar is dissolved. Cook, covered, over medium heat for 2 to 3 minutes or until steam washes sugar crystals from side of pan. Cook, uncovered, to 234° to 240° on candy thermometer, soft-ball stage. Stir in vinegar. Cook for 1 minute longer. Stir in pecans. Drop into 3-inch circles on buttered waxed paper. Let stand until firm. Yield: 2 dozen.

PECAN PIE

1 cup chopped pecans	1 tablespoon melted butter
1 unbaked 9-inch pie shell	1/2 teaspoon vanilla extract
3 eggs	1 tablespoon flour
1 cup light corn syrup	1 cup sugar

Sprinkle pecans in pie shell. Beat eggs in bowl. Add corn syrup, melted butter and vanilla; mix well. Add mixture of flour and sugar. Pour over pecans. Let stand until pecans rise to top. Bake at 350° F. for 45 minutes. Yield: 6 servings.

TARTA DE PACANAS

1 taza de pacanas picadas	1 cucharada de mantequilla
1 costra para tarta, de 9	derretida
pulgadas, sin hornear	1/2 cucharadita de vainilla
3 huevos	1 cucharada de harina
1 taza de miel de maíz	1 taza de azúcar

Ponga las pacanas en la costra. Bata los huevos en una vasija. Añada miel de maíz, mantequilla y vainilla; mezcle bien. Añada una mezcla de harina y azúcar. Vierta encima de las pacanas. Deje hasta que las pacanas suban. Hornee a 350° F. por 45 minutos.

ANISEED COOKIES (GALLETITAS DE ANISE) — Mexico

2 cups sugar	3 cups flour
4 eggs	Aniseed

Combine sugar and eggs in mixer bowl. Beat for 20 minutes. Add flour gradually, beating constantly. Shape into dough. Roll 3/8 inch thick on floured surface. Cut as desired. Grease cookie sheet generously. Sprinkle with aniseed. Place cookies 1 inch apart on prepared cookie sheet. Chill in refrigerator for 6 to 8 hours. Bake at 325° F. until light brown. Remove to wire rack to cool. Yield: 6 dozen.

BROWNIES

1 cup sugar	1 tablespoon vanilla extract
3 tablespoons baking cocoa	3/4 cup flour
2 eggs, beaten	3 tablespoons butter, softened

Mix sugar and cocoa in bowl. Blend in eggs and vanilla. Add flour and butter; mix well. Pour into greased 8 x 8-inch baking pan. Bake at 350° F. for 30 minutes. Cool slightly. Cut into bars. Yield: 10 servings.

BARRITAS DE CHOCOLATE

1 taza de azúcar	3/4 taza de harina
3 cucharadas de cacao en polvo	3 cucharadas de mantequilla
2 huevos batidos	suavizada
1 cucharadita de vainilla	

Mezcle el azúcar y el cacao en una vasija. Añada los huevos y la vainilla; bata hasta cremosa. Agregue la harina y la mantequilla; mezcle bien. Ponga en un molde engrasado de 8 por 8 pulgadas. Hornee a 350° F. por 30 minutos. Enfríese un poco. Corte en barritas.

BUÑUELOS

3¹/₃ cups flour
1¹/₂ tablespoons sugar
1 teaspoon baking powder
1 teaspoon salt
¹/₄ cup butter

2 eggs
¹/₄ cup milk
Oil for deep frying
1 cup sugar
Cinnamon to taste

Sift flour, 1¹/₂ tablespoons sugar, baking powder and salt into bowl. Add butter. Rub in butter with fingers until mixture is the consistency of coarse meal. Add mixture of eggs and milk; mix to form dough. Knead lightly on floured surface for 2 minutes or until smooth. Shape into 1-inch balls. Let rest for 15 minutes. Roll each ball into 4-inch circle. Cut small circle in center. Deep-fry in hot oil for 30 seconds on each side or until puffed and golden. Drain on paper towel. Place 1 at a time in paper bag with mixture of 1 cup sugar and cinnamon; shake gently to coat well. Yield: 6 dozen.

BISCOCHOS — Mexico

2 cups shortening
³/₄ cup sugar
1 tablespoon cinnamon
6 cups flour

2 tablespoons baking powder
1 tablespoon salt
³/₄ cup fruit juice or water
1 teaspoon anise flavoring

Cream shortening in mixer bowl until light. Add sugar and cinnamon, beating until fluffy. Add mixture of flour, baking powder and salt alternately with juice, mixing well after each addition. Mix in anise flavoring. Drop onto cookie sheet. Bake at 400° F. for 12 to 14 minutes or until light brown. Yield: 6 to 8 dozen.

POWDER COOKIES (POLOVORONES) — Mexico

1 cup butter, softened
¹/₂ cup confectioners' sugar

2¹/₂ cups sifted flour
¹/₂ teaspoon vanilla extract

Cream butter and confectioners' sugar in mixer bowl until light and fluffy. Add flour and vanilla; mix well. Chill for 5 hours. Roll on floured surface. Cut into 1-inch cookies. Place on greased cookie sheet. Bake at 400° F. for 15 minutes. Dust with additional confectioners' sugar while hot. Remove to wire rack to cool. Yield: 2 1/2 dozen.

CHOCOLATE CHIP COOKIES

2¹/4 cups flour
1 teaspoon soda
1 teaspoon salt
1 cup butter, softened
³/4 cup sugar

³/4 cup packed brown sugar
2 eggs
1 6-ounce package chocolate
   chips

Mix flour, soda and salt in small bowl. Cream butter and sugars in mixer bowl until light. Blend in eggs. Add flour mixture; mix well. Stir in chocolate chips. Drop by spoonfuls onto greased cookie sheet. Bake at 375° F. for 10 minutes. Cool on wire rack. Yield: 3 dozen.

GALLETAS CON PEDACITOS DE CHOCOLATE

2¹/4 tazas de harina
1 cucharadita de bicarbonato
   de soda
1 cucharadita de sal
1 taza de mantequilla
   suavizada

³/4 taza de azúcar
³/4 taza de azúcar moreno muy
   compacto
1 paquete de pedacitos de
   chocolate
2 huevos

Mezcle la harina, bicarbonato de soda y sal. Combine la mantequilla y los azúcares en una vasija; bata bien hasta que se ponga cremosa. Añada los huevos; bata bien. Añada gradualmente la harina; mezcle todo bien. Añada los pedacitos de chocolate. Ponga por cucharadas en una hoja de lámina engrasada. Hornee a 375° F. por 10 minutos.

ORANGE COOKIES

1 tablespoon grated orange rind
1 tablespoon boiling water
¹/2 cup shortening
¹/2 cup sugar

1 egg
2 cups flour
2 tablespoons orange juice

Combine orange rind with boiling water in cup. Let stand for several minutes. Cream shortening and sugar in mixer bowl until light and fluffy. Beat in egg and orange rind. Add flour alternately with orange juice, mixing well after each addition. Roll ¹/8 inch thick on floured surface. Cut with 2-inch cookie cutter. Place on greased cookie sheet. Bake at 375° F. for 8 minutes or until golden. Remove to wire rack to cool. Yield: 3¹/2 dozen.

TEA COOKIES

1 cup butter, softened
2 cups flour
1/4 cup confectioners' sugar

2 cups chopped pecans
2 teaspoons vanilla extract

Combine all ingredients in bowl; mix well. Shape into small balls. Place on baking sheet. Bake at 300° F. until golden brown. Roll in additional confectioners' sugar while hot. Cool. Roll in confectioners' sugar again.
Yield: 4 dozen.

PASTELITOS PARA EL TÉ

1 taza de mantequilla
    suavizada
2 tazas de harina

1/4 taza de azúcar en polvo
2 tazas de pacanas picadas
2 cucharaditas de vainilla

Mezcle bien los ingredientes en una vasija. Haga bolitas de masa. Póngalas en una hoja engrasada de hornear. Hornee a 300° F. hasta que se doren. Háganse rodar por el azúcar en polvo mientras estén todavía calientes. Enfríese y ruédese otra vez en azúcar.

WEDDING COOKIES — Mexico

6 egg yolks
1 cup shortening
2 cups sifted flour

1 cup sugar
2 tablespoons cinnamon
Confectioners' sugar

Beat egg yolks and shortening in bowl until well blended. Add sifted dry ingredients gradually, mixing well after each addition. Shape into small balls. Place 1 inch apart on greased cookie sheet. Press lightly to flatten. Bake at 350° F. for 8 to 10 minutes or until light brown. Roll in confectioners' sugar.
Yield: 8 dozen.

PIÑA COLADA COOKIES

1/4 cup butter, softened
8 ounces cream cheese,
    softened
1 egg yolk
1/2 cup pineapple juice

1/2 teaspoon rum extract
1 2-layer package yellow cake
    mix
1 cup coconut

Cream butter and cream cheese in mixer bowl until light and fluffy. Blend in egg yolk, pineapple juice and rum extract. Add cake mix 1/3 at a time, mixing well after each addition. Stir in coconut. Chill, covered, for 30 minutes. Drop by teaspoonfuls onto ungreased cookie sheet. Bake at 375° F. for 11 minutes or until light brown. Cool on cookie sheet for several minutes. Remove to wire rack to cool completely. Yield: 4 dozen.

COCONUT TRIFLE — Venezuela

3/4 cup grape juice or Muscatel
1 sponge cake, cut into pieces
1 coconut
2 cups hot water

1 cup sugar
1 2-inch cinnamon stick
6 egg yolks

Pour grape juice over cake in dessert dish. Pierce coconut; drain. Break open coconut. Remove and peel coconut meat with sharp knife. Grate meat; place in fine strainer. Pour hot water over coconut; let drain for 15 minutes, collecting liquid in bowl. Press to extract 2 cups liquid. Combine 1 1/2 cups liquid with sugar and cinnamon stick in saucepan. Bring to a boil over medium heat, stirring to dissolve sugar. Cook to 234° to 240° on candy thermometer, soft-ball stage. Remove from heat; discard cinnamon stick. Beat egg yolks in bowl until thick and lemon-colored. Add remaining 1/2 cup coconut liquid and 3 tablespoons hot syrup, beating constantly. Stir egg yolks into hot syrup. Cook over low heat until thickened, stirring constantly. Do not boil. Pour over cake. Chill for 3 hours. Garnish with cinnamon, grated coconut and raisins. Yield: 6 to 8 servings.

ANGEL SWEET

6 ounces semisweet chocolate,
   melted
2 tablespoons melted butter
1 egg

1 cup confectioners' sugar
1 cup chopped pecans
2 cups miniature marshmallows
1/2 cup shredded coconut

Blend chocolate and butter in bowl. Add egg; mix well. Mix in confectioners' sugar, pecans and marshmallows. Shape into 1-inch balls. Roll in coconut. Chill. Yield: 4 dozen.

DULCE DE ÁNGEL

6 onzas de chocolate
   semidulce, derretido
2 cucharadas de mantequilla
   derretida
1 huevo
1 taza de azúcar en polvo,
   cernido

1 taza de nueces picadas
2 tazas de malvaviscos
   pequeños
1/2 taza de coco rallado

Mezcle el chocolate y la mantequilla en una olla. Añada el huevo; mezcle bien. Añada el azúcar, nueces y malvaviscos. Forme bolitas de 1 pulgada; ruede en el coco. Enfríese.

BANANAS CABANA

6 bananas
1/4 cup butter
1/2 cup packed brown sugar
Cinnamon to taste

1/2 cup orange juice
2 tablespoons orange liqueur
6 scoops vanilla ice cream

Cut bananas into halves lengthwise. Melt butter in skillet. Add bananas. Sauté for several minutes on each side or until golden. Sprinkle with brown sugar and cinnamon. Add orange juice. Simmer for 1 minute. Pour orange liqueur over top; ignite. Let flames subside. Serve over ice cream in dessert dishes. Yield: 6 servings.

BREAD PUDDING (CAPIROTADA) — Mexico

3/4 cup packed brown sugar
3/4 cup water
1/2 teaspoon cinnamon
21/2 cups bread cubes

1/2 cup shredded Cheddar
cheese
3/4 cup raisins
3/4 cup chopped walnuts

Bring brown sugar, water and cinnamon to a boil in saucepan; reduce heat. Cook until brown sugar is dissolved, stirring constantly. Pour over bread cubes in bowl. Toss to mix well. Add cheese, raisins and walnuts. Spoon into buttered 11/2-quart baking dish. Bake at 375° F. for 15 minutes or until cheese is melted. Serve warm with sweetened whipped cream or ice cream. Yield: 6 servings.

CARROT PUDDING (PUDIN DE ZANAHORIA) — Mexico

1 cup grated carrot
1 tablespoon lemon juice
1/2 teaspoon grated lemon rind
3 tablespoons butter, softened
1/2 cup sugar

4 eggs, beaten
2 tablespoons flour
1/4 teaspoon salt
3/4 teaspoon vanilla extract

Combine carrot, lemon juice and lemon rind in bowl. Let stand for 10 minutes. Cream butter and sugar in mixer bowl until light and fluffy. Blend in eggs. Add flour, salt, vanilla and carrot mixture; mix well. Spoon into buttered baking dish. Bake at 350° F. for 20 minutes or until set and golden brown. Yield: 4 servings.

FLAN — Mexico

1/2 cup sugar
5 eggs
6 cups milk

1 cup sugar
1 teaspoon vanilla extract
1/4 teaspoon salt

Sprinkle 1/2 cup sugar in small skillet. Heat until sugar melts and forms a light brown syrup. Pour into 2-quart mold, rotating to spread evenly; cool. Beat eggs in bowl. Add remaining ingredients; mix well. Pour into prepared mold. Set in larger pan of water. Bake at 350° F. for 30 minutes or until knife inserted in center comes out clean. Yield: 8 servings

PINEAPPLE PUDDING (QUESILLO) — Mexico

3 cups pineapple juice
3 cups sugar

12 eggs
1/2 cup raisins

Combine pineapple juice and sugar in saucepan. Cook until reduced to 2 cups. Beat eggs in bowl until thick and lemon-colored. Add 1 cup syrup and raisins. Pour into 2-quart mold. Place in larger pan of hot water. Bake at 350° F. for 1 hour. Cool. Remove to serving plate. Pour remaining 1 cup syrup over pudding. Garnish with fresh pineapple. Yield: 8 servings.

LEMON PARFAITS (PARFAITS DE LIMÓN) — Mexico

1 1/2 cups sugar
1 cup water
Thinly sliced peel of 1 lemon
3 egg whites

1/4 cup lemon juice
2 cups whipping cream,
   whipped

Combine sugar, water and lemon peel in saucepan. Cook to 230° to 234° on candy thermometer, spun-thread stage. Beat egg whites in bowl until soft peaks form. Add hot syrup gradually, beating constantly. Cool. Fold in lemon juice and whipped cream. Spoon into freezer container. Freeze until firm, stirring several times. Spoon into parfait glasses. Garnish with fresh flower. Yield: 8 servings.

SWEET TURNOVERS — Mexico

1 recipe 2-crust pie pastry
1 cup crushed pineapple

1/2 cup coconut
Confectioners' sugar

Roll pastry thin on floured surface. Cut into 3-inch circles. Mix pineapple and coconut in bowl. Spoon a small amount of fruit mixture onto each circle. Fold pastry over to enclose filling. Moisten and seal edges. Place on baking sheet. Bake at 400° F. for 15 to 18 minutes or until brown. Sprinkle with confectioners' sugar. May deep-fry in hot oil if preferred. May fill with fruit preserves or mixture of 1 cup thick applesauce and 1/4 cup chopped nuts. Yield: 8 servings.

GLOBAL SAMPLER

SANGRIA PUNCH — Spain

1 12-ounce can frozen grape
   juice concentrate
1 12-ounce can frozen pink
   lemonade concentrate

2 quarts ginger ale
Orange slices

Combine juices and ginger ale in pitcher. Pour over ice in punch cups. Place orange slice in each cup. Yield: 25 servings.

SANGRÍA SIN VINO — España

1 lata de 12 onzas de jugo de
   uvas congelado
1 lata de 12 onzas de limonada
   rosa congelado

2 litros de ginger ale
Rebanadas de naranja

Mezcle los jugos y el ginger ale en una jarra. Sirva sobre cubitos de hielo en vasos. Ponga una rebanada de naranja en cada vaso.

SPICED COFFEE — Austria

4¹/2 cups water
6 tablespoons coffee
4 cinnamon sticks
8 whole cloves

8 whole allspice
¹/2 cup whipping cream,
   whipped
Nutmeg

Pour water into electric coffee maker. Place coffee, cinnamon sticks, cloves and allspice in basket. Brew coffee. Pour into small cups. Top with whipped cream. Sprinkle with nutmeg. Serve with sugar. Yield: 8 servings.

GAZPACHO — Spain

3 medium tomatoes	2 tablespoons vinegar
1 small onion	2 tablespoons olive oil
1 red or green pepper	1 teaspoon salt
1 clove of garlic	Bread
4 cups tomato juice	1 medium cucumber

Peel tomatoes. Chop tomatoes, onion, pepper and garlic. Combine with tomato juice, vinegar, olive oil and salt in blender. Process for 1 or 2 minutes, adding a small amount of bread to thicken mixture. Chill for 2 hours. Chop cucumber. Serve soup with cucumber. Yield: 10 servings.

GAZPACHO — España

3 tomates medianos	2 cucharadas de vinagre
1 cebolla pequeña	2 cucharadas de aceite de oliva
1 pimiento rojo o verde	1 cucharadita de sal
1 diente de ajo	Pan
4 tazas de jugo de tomate	1 pepino mediano

Pele los tomates. Pique los tomates, la cebolla, el pimiento y el ajo. Póngase en una licuadora con el jugo de tomate, vinagre, aceite de oliva y sal. Licúe durante 1 ó 2 minutos con un poco de pan para espesarlo. Ponga la sopa a enfriar en el regrigerador durante 2 horas. Corte el pepino en cubitas. Sirva la sopa con el pepino. 10 porciones.

BEET SOUP (BORSCH) — Russia

2 onions, chopped	2 carrots, shredded
2 stalks celery, chopped	3/4 cup chopped potato
1/4 cup butter	5 beets, chopped
8 cups beef bouillon	1 tablespoon lemon juice
1/2 cabbage, shredded	Salt and pepper to taste

Sauté onions and celery in butter in saucepan. Add bouillon. Bring to a boil. Add remaining vegetables, lemon juice and seasonings. Simmer for 30 minutes or just until vegetables are tender. Ladle into soup bowls. Serve with dollop of sour cream. Yield: 6 to 8 servings.

LEMON SOUP (SOUPA AVGOLEMONO) — Greece

4 pieces chicken
1 carrot, chopped
1 stalk celery, chopped
2 onions, cut into quarters

1/2 cup rice
Salt to taste
2 egg yolks
Juice of 1 lemon

Combine chicken, vegetables and water to cover in saucepan. Cook until chicken is tender. Remove and chop chicken. Strain broth. Combine rice with broth in saucepan. Cook just until rice is tender. Season to taste. Beat egg yolks and lemon juice in bowl. Whisk a small amount of hot soup into egg mixture; whisk egg mixture into soup. Add chicken. Heat just to serving temperature. Ladle into soup bowls. Garnish with slice of lemon. Yield: 4 servings.

AUTUMN SALAD — Sweden

1 pound plums
2 apples, chopped
2 potatoes, cooked, chopped
1 carrot, sliced, cooked
2 stalks celery, sliced, cooked
2 dill pickles, chopped
4 ounces cooked ham, chopped

4 ounces beef brisket, boiled,
   chopped
1/4 cup chopped walnuts
1/2 cup mayonnaise
1/4 cup sour cream
Juice of 1 lemon
1 head lettuce, torn

Scald plums. Remove skins and pits. Combine with apples, potatoes, carrot, celery, pickles, ham, beef and walnuts in serving bowl; mix lightly. Mix mayonnaise, sour cream and lemon juice in small bowl. Add mayonnaise mixture and lettuce to salad; toss lightly to mix. Chill until serving time. Yield: 10 servings.

BULGUR AND PARSLEY SALAD (TABBULI) — Lebanon

3/4 cup bulgur
4 cups chopped fresh parsley
1 cup chopped fresh mint
6 green onions, chopped
2 tomatoes, chopped

2 tablespoons dried onion
1/2 cup lemon juice
1/8 teaspoon cinnamon
Salt and pepper to taste
1/2 cup olive oil

Rinse bulgur; drain well, pressing out water. Place in large serving bowl. Layer parsley, mint, green onions and tomatoes over bulgur. Mix dried onion with lemon juice and seasonings in small bowl. Add olive oil. Pour over layers; toss to mix well. Yield: 8 servings.

CUCUMBER SALAD (CACIK) — Turkey

2 cucumbers	2 cups yogurt
1 teaspoon salt	3 tablespoons olive oil
1 tablespoon vinegar	1 teaspoon chopped dill leaves
1 clove of garlic, crushed	1 teaspoon chopped mint

Peel cucumbers. Cut into quarters lengthwise; slice paper-thin. Sprinkle with salt. Let stand for 15 minutes. Combine vinegar and garlic in cup. Let stand for 10 minutes. Combine yogurt, olive oil and dill leaves in serving bowl. Strain vinegar into yogurt mixture. Drain cucumbers. Add to yogurt; mix well. Sprinkle with mint. Chill until serving time. Yield: 4 servings.

SESAME CHICKEN SALAD — China

4 chicken breasts	1 tablespoon soy sauce
6 cups water	1 tablespoon oil
1 tablespoon soy sauce	1 tablespoon sesame oil
$1/2$ teaspoon salt	$1/4$ teaspoon ginger
$1/2$ teaspoon 5-spice powder	$1/8$ teaspoon pepper
3 stalks celery, diagonally sliced	1 tablespoon toasted sesame seed

Combine chicken, water, 1 tablespoon soy sauce, salt and 5-spice powder in 3-quart saucepan. Simmer, covered, for 20 minutes or until chicken is tender; remove from heat. Let stand for 1 hour. Remove chicken; cut chicken into $1/2$-inch slices. Bring chicken broth to a boil. Add celery. Cook for 2 minutes or just until tender-crisp; drain. Toss chicken, celery, 1 tablespoon soy sauce, oils, ginger and pepper in serving dish. Sprinkle with sesame seed. Yield: 4 servings.

VEGETABLE SALAD (GADO-GADO) — Indonesia

$1/2$ head cabbage, shredded	1 tablespoon cayenne pepper
8 ounces green beans, broken	1 cup oil
1 head lettuce	1 cup water
4 tomatoes, sliced	2 tablespoons peanut butter
$1/2$ cucumber, sliced	1 teaspoon sugar
5 potatoes, boiled, sliced	2 tablespoons soy sauce
3 onions, sliced	Juice of 1 lemon
4 hard-boiled eggs, sliced	Grated rind of 1 lemon

Cook cabbage and beans separately in water to cover in saucepans until tender-crisp. Rinse with cold water; drain. Place lettuce leaves on serving platter. Arrange cabbage, beans, tomatoes, cucumber, potatoes, onions and eggs on lettuce. Brown cayenne pepper in oil in saucepan. Stir in water. Add peanut butter, sugar, soy sauce, lemon juice, and lemon rind; mix well. Drizzle over salad. Yield: 8 servings.

BEEF STROGANOFF — Russia

8 ounces fresh mushrooms, sliced	Flour
1 large onion, sliced	2 tablespoons butter
2 tablespoons butter	Salt and pepper to taste
2 pounds round steak	1 can beef bouillon
	1 cup sour cream

Sauté mushrooms and onion in 2 tablespoons butter in saucepan. Remove with slotted spoon. Cut steak into 3/4 x 2-inch strips. Roll in flour, coating well. Add 2 tablespoons butter and steak to saucepan. Cook until beef is brown. Season to taste. Add enough water to bouillon to measure 2 cups. Add to saucepan. Simmer for 1 1/2 hours or until tender, stirring occasionally. Stir in mushrooms, onion and sour cream. Heat to serving temperature. Serve over noodles. Yield: 6 servings.

STIR-FRIED BEEF AND VEGETABLES — China

1 1/2 tablespoons Argo cornstarch	1 tablespoon white vinegar
1 tablespoon brown sugar	3/4 cup beef broth
1/2 teaspoon minced fresh ginger	2 tablespoons dry Sherry
1 clove of garlic, minced	1/4 cup Mazola corn oil
Pinch of red pepper	2 cups broccoli flowerets
2 tablespoons soy sauce	1 cup sliced mushrooms
	1 pound lean beef, thinly sliced
	16 cherry tomato halves

Combine first 7 ingredients in 1-pint jar. Cover and shake until well mixed. Add beef broth and Sherry. Heat oil in wok over medium heat. Add broccoli and mushrooms. Stir-fry for 1 minute. Remove with slotted spoon. Add beef. Stir-fry for 1 to 2 minutes. Add vegetables and broth mixture. Cook for 1 minute, stirring constantly. Add cherry tomatoes. Serve over rice. May store cooking sauce in refrigerator for up to 2 weeks or freeze for longer periods. Yield: 4 servings.

Photograph for this recipe on Cover.

VEAL NUGGETS PAPRIKA (BORJÚPAPRIKÁS) — Hungary

1¹/₂ pounds ground veal
1 cup bread crumbs
¹/₂ cup milk
¹/₄ cup minced onion
¹/₄ teaspoon Tabasco sauce
¹/₄ teaspoon chervil
¹/₄ teaspoon tarragon

¹/₂ teaspoon salt
2 tablespoons flour
2 cups sour cream
¹/₂ teaspoon salt
¹/₂ cup milk
1 tablespoon paprika

Combine ground veal, bread crumbs, milk, onion, Tabasco sauce, chervil, tarragon and ¹/₂ teaspoon salt in bowl. Shape into 1-inch balls. Drop into salted boiling water in saucepan. Cook for 10 to 12 minutes; drain. Blend flour, sour cream and ¹/₂ teaspoon salt in saucepan. Stir in milk and paprika. Cook until thickened, stirring constantly. Add meatballs. Heat to serving temperature; do not boil. Serve over noodles. Yield: 4 servings.

Photograph for this recipe on page 4.

LAMB AND CABBAGE — Norway

1¹/₂ pounds breast of lamb
2 pounds cabbage
2 to 3 teaspoons salt
10 peppercorns

8 potatoes
8 carrots
1 tablespoon chopped parsley
Melted butter

Cut lamb into serving pieces. Slice cabbage. Alternate layers of lamb and cabbage in saucepan, sprinkling layers with salt. Sprinkle with peppercorns. Add water to cover. Bring to a boil; skim off foam. Reduce heat. Simmer, covered, for 30 minutes to 1¹/₂ hours or until tender. Cook potatoes and carrots in water in saucepan until tender. Place lamb and cabbage on serving plate. Arrange potatoes and carrots on plate. Sprinkle with parsley. Serve with butter. Yield: 4 servings.

LAMB WITH ROSEMARY — Australia

4 ounces onions, sliced
2 tablespoons chopped celery
¹/₂ cup chicken stock
1 pound lamb chops, trimmed
¹/₈ teaspoon thyme

¹/₄ teaspoon rosemary
1¹/₂ cups chicken stock
Salt and pepper to taste
2 medium potatoes, parboiled,
    sliced

Cook onions and celery in 1/2 cup chicken stock in saucepan until tender. Place in baking dish. Grill lamb chops 3 inches from coals for 5 minutes on each side or until brown. Place in baking dish. Sprinkle with thyme and rosemary. Add remaining 11/2 cups stock. Season with salt and pepper to taste. Top with sliced potatoes. Bake at 350° F. for 20 minutes or until potatoes are brown.
Yield: 2 servings.

CHRISTMAS HAM — Sweden

1 cooked ham	1 bay leaf
4 cups water	1 egg white
1 onion, cut into quarters	1 tablespoon dry mustard
1 carrot, sliced	1 tablespoon sugar
10 peppercorns	1 cup fine bread crumbs
1/2 teaspoon cloves	

Place ham in large roasting pan with fatty side up. Add water, onion, carrot, peppercorns, cloves and bay leaf. Bake at 350° F. for 1 hour. Replace water which has evaporated; turn ham. Bake for 1 hour longer. Remove rind and most of the fat from ham. Chill fatty side up in liquid overnight. Brush with mixture of egg white, dry mustard and sugar. Sprinkle with bread crumbs. Bake at 450° F. for 45 minutes or until golden brown. Garnish with prunes and applesauce. Serve with red cabbage.

SPICED PORK SPIT — Australia

1 tablespoon wine vinegar	3/4 teaspoon pepper
1/2 cup olive oil	11/2 pounds boneless pork
1 teaspoon mustard	shoulder
2 tablespoons chopped onion	3 tomatoes
1 teaspoon sugar	3 apples
1/2 teaspoon allspice	8 ounces mushrooms
2 teaspoons salt	

Bring vinegar, olive oil, mustard, onion, sugar and seasonings to a boil in saucepan; cool. Cut pork into large cubes. Add to oil mixture. Let stand for 1 hour or longer. Slice tomatoes and apples into thick slices. Drain pork, reserving marinade. Thread pork, tomatoes, apples and mushrooms on skewers. Grill over hot coals until pork is well done, brushing occasionally with marinade.
Yield: 4 to 6 servings.

SWEET AND SOUR PORK — China

1/4 cup soy sauce
11/2 tablespoons dry Sherry
2 teaspoons sugar
1 egg yolk
11/2 pounds lean pork cubes
1/2 cup cornstarch
Oil for deep frying
3 tablespoons oil
1 onion, thinly sliced
8 green onions, diagonally
  sliced
1 green pepper, coarsely
  chopped
2 stalks celery, diagonally
  sliced
1 cucumber, sliced
1 20-ounce can pineapple
  chunks
1/4 cup vinegar
3 tablespoons tomato sauce
1 cup water
2 tablespoons cornstarch

Combine soy sauce, Sherry, sugar and egg yolk in bowl; mix well. Add pork. Let stand for 1 hour, stirring occasionally. Drain pork, reserving marinade. Roll pork in 1/2 cup cornstarch, coating well. Deep-fry 1/2 at a time in 375° oil for 5 minutes or until golden brown. Drain on paper towel. Heat 3 tablespoons oil in wok over high heat. Stir-fry vegetables in hot oil for 5 minutes. Drain pineapple, reserving syrup. Add reserved pineapple syrup, reserved marinade, vinegar and tomato sauce to wok. Stir in mixture of water and 2 tablespoons cornstarch. Cook until thickened, stirring constantly. Stir in pork and pineapple. Serve with rice. Yield: 6 servings.

PORK AND RICE PILAF
(HERINON KAI REZI PALIF) — Greece

8 ounces chopped pork
1 onion, chopped
3 slices bacon, chopped
1 cup rice
Salt and pepper to taste
2 cups hot water
2 small sweet red peppers,
  chopped
1/2 cup cooked green peas

Brown pork and onion with bacon in saucepan, stirring constantly. Add rice, salt and pepper. Sauté for several minutes; drain. Stir in hot water and red peppers. Bring to a boil; reduce heat. Simmer, covered, until rice is tender. Stir in peas. Yield: 4 servings.

CASHEW CHICKEN — China

4 chicken breast filets
2 teaspoons soy sauce
1 teaspoon cornstarch
2 tablespoons oil
1 small onion, chopped
1/2 cup snow peas
1/2 cup chopped broccoli

1/2 cup parboiled cut green
  beans
1 tablespoon cornstarch
2 tablespoons soy sauce
1/4 cup chicken broth
1 cup roasted cashews

Cut chicken into 1-inch cubes. Combine with 2 teaspoons soy sauce and 1 teaspoon cornstarch in bowl. Marinate for 20 minutes. Heat tablespoon oil to 375° in wok. Add chicken. Stir-fry for 2 to 3 minutes or until brown. Push to 1 side. Add remaining 1 tablespoon oil and onion. Stir-fry for 1 minute. Add remaining vegetables. Stir-fry until tender-crisp. Stir in chicken. Combine 1 tablespoon cornstarch, 2 tablespoons soy sauce and chicken broth in bowl. Stir into chicken mixture. Cook until thickened, stirring constantly. Stir in cashews. Serve with rice. Garnish with green onions. Yield: 4 servings.

CHICKEN WITH RICE (ARROZ CON POLLO) — Spain

1 chicken
1 medium onion, chopped
Salt and pepper to taste
5 cups water
1 large onion, chopped

2 green peppers, chopped
2 tablespoons chicken fat
8 ounces peeled shrimp,
  chopped
1 cup rice

Combine chicken, 1 medium onion, salt and pepper in water in saucepan. Cook until chicken is tender. Drain, reserving 3 cups broth. Chop chicken, discarding skin and bones. Sauté 1 large onion and green peppers in chicken fat in heavy saucepan. Add chopped chicken, shrimp, reserved broth and rice. Bring to a boil over high heat; reduce heat. Simmer, covered, for 20 minutes. Remove from heat. Let stand for 5 minutes. Yield: 6 servings.

CHICKEN AND PEANUT STEW — Africa

2 chickens, cut up	2 potatoes, chopped
6 cups water	2 eggplant, seeded, chopped
1¹/₂ cups unsalted peanuts	Salt and pepper to taste
2 onions, minced	

Combine chickens with 6 cups water in heavy saucepan. Cook for 30 minutes. Add peanuts, onions, potatoes, eggplant, seasonings and enough water to cover. Simmer, covered, for 30 minutes or until tender. Serve over egg yolk and rice in individual serving bowls. Serve with sliced bananas and chutney.
Yield: 4 servings.

SWISS CHICKEN (POULET À LA SUISSE) — Switzerland

6 chicken breast filets	6 tablespoons margarine
6 slices Swiss cheese	¹/₂ cup dry white wine
6 slices cooked ham	1 cube chicken bouillon
3 tablespoons flour	1 tablespoon cornstarch
1 teaspoon paprika	1 cup heavy cream

Pound chicken with meat mallet until thin. Place 1 slice cheese and 1 slice ham on each fillet. Roll to enclose filling; secure with toothpicks. Coat with mixture of flour and paprika. Brown in margarine in skillet. Add wine and bouillon. Simmer, covered, for 30 to 50 minutes or until tender. Remove to serving plate. Stir mixture of cornstarch and cream into skillet. Cook until thickened, stirring constantly. Spoon over chicken. Yield: 6 servings.

CHICKEN CURRY — India

1 5-pound chicken	1 teaspoon ginger
1 small onion, chopped	1 tablespoon curry powder
3 tablespoons butter	1 cup milk
3 tablespoons flour	Salt to taste

Cook chicken in water to cover in saucepan until tender. Remove and chop chicken. Reserve 2 cups broth. Sauté onion in butter in saucepan. Sprinkle with flour, ginger and curry powder. Stir in milk and reserved broth. Cook until thickened, stirring constantly. Add chicken and salt. Heat to serving temperature. Serve over rice with small bowls of raisins, sieved egg yolks, sieved egg whites, chopped peanuts, toasted coconut and chutney. Yield: 8 to 10 servings.

SALMON LOAF (COULIBIAC) —Turkey

1 16-ounce can salmon
1/2 cup chopped onion
2 tablespoons butter
3/4 cup sliced mushrooms
2 tablespoons dry white wine
3 tablespoons chopped
   dillweed
2 teaspoons lemon juice
1/2 teaspoon salt

1/4 teaspoon pepper
3 cups cooked rice
1 10-ounce package frozen
   chopped spinach, cooked,
   drained
2 hard-boiled eggs, chopped
2 sheets frozen puff pastry,
   thawed
1 egg, beaten

Drain salmon, reserving liquid. Sauté onion in butter in saucepan just until transparent. Add mushrooms. Sauté for 3 minutes. Stir in salmon liquid, wine, dillweed, lemon juice, salt and pepper. Add salmon and rice; mix well. Mix spinach and hard-boiled eggs in bowl. Roll 1 sheet of pastry into 10 x 12-inch rectangle on floured surface. Mound half the salmon mixture onto center of pastry, leaving 3-inch edge on all sides. Arrange half the spinach on salmon mixture. Bring up pastry to enclose filling; seal edges. Place seam side down on baking sheet. Brush with beaten egg. Repeat with remaining ingredients. Bake at 350° F. until brown. Yield: 8 servings.

Photograph for this recipe on page 122.

FRIED FISH AND RICE (KEDGEREE) — India

1 pound saltwater fish
1 onion, sliced
Salt and pepper to taste
3/4 cup long grain rice
2 cups water
2 onions, chopped

2 cloves of garlic, minced
1 tablespoon turmeric
2 hard-boiled eggs, sliced
2 tomatoes, sliced
1 green pepper, cut into strips
1/2 cup green peas

Combine fish with sliced onion, salt and pepper to taste and water to cover in saucepan. Cook for 10 minutes. Drain and cool fish. Combine rice with 2 cups water and salt to taste in saucepan. Cook for 15 minutes or until rice is tender and liquid is absorbed. Sauté chopped onions and garlic in butter in skillet just until transparent. Add turmeric, fish and rice. Sauté until light brown. Spoon into serving dish. Top with hard-boiled eggs, tomatoes, green pepper and peas. Yield: 4 servings.

FRIED SQUID — Spain

3 pounds small squid
1/4 cup olive oil
Juice of 1 lemon
Flour

Salt
2 eggs
Olive oil for deep frying

Wash squid well. Remove skin, eyes and spine. Cut into small pieces. Place in mixture of 1/4 cup olive oil and lemon juice in bowl. Marinate for 1 hour; drain. Dip in mixture of flour and salt, then in eggs and then in flour again. Deep-fry in olive oil until brown. Yield: 4 servings.

CALAMARES FRITOS — España

11/2 kilogramos de calamares
    pequeños
1/4 taza de aceite de oliva
Jugo de 1 limón

Harina
Sal
2 huevos
Aceite de oliva para freír

Lave los calamares. Limpie bien y quite el pellejo, los ojos y la espina. Corte en pedazos pequeños. Ponga los pedazos a remojar en 1/4 taza de aceite y jugo de limón por una hora; escurra. Cubra cada pedazo con una mezcla de harina y sal, luego huevo y otra vez harina. Fríalos en aceite de oliva muy caliente.

POACHED SALMON WITH DILL HOLLANDAISE (KOKT LAX MED HOLLANDÄSSÅS) — Sweden

2 tablespoons wine vinegar
1/2 cup dry white wine
1 cup water
1 teaspoon dillweed
7 white peppercorns
5 whole allspice
1 bay leaf
2 teaspoons salt

8 salmon steaks
4 egg yolks
1/2 cup butter
3 tablespoons boiling water
3 tablespoons lemon juice
1/2 teaspoon dillweed
1/2 teaspoon salt

Combine vinegar, wine, 1 cup water, 1 teaspoon dillweed, peppercorns, allspice, bay leaf and 2 teaspoons salt in large skillet. Add salmon. Poach, covered, just until fish flakes easily. Beat egg yolks in bowl until thick and lemon-colored. Combine butter, 3 tablespoons boiling water, lemon juice, 1/2 teaspoon dillweed and 1/2 teaspoon salt in double boiler. Bring just to the simmering point. Stir a small of hot mixture into egg yolks; stir egg yolks into hot mixture. Cook until thickened, stirring constantly. Remove salmon to serving platter. Spoon a small amount of the sauce over salmon. Garnish with watercress. Pass remaining sauce. Yield: 8 servings.

SHRIMP AND SPINACH OMELET (KANOKOYAKI) — Japan

8 ounces peeled shrimp	1/2 teaspoon sugar
1/2 cup oil	1 teaspoon soy sauce
1 tablespoon vinegar	1/2 teaspoon salt
4 eggs	8 ounces chopped spinach
1 cup chicken or fish bouillon	

Combine shrimp with 1/2 cup oil and vinegar in bowl. Let stand for several minutes. Beat eggs with bouillon, sugar, soy sauce and salt in bowl. Heat a small amount of oil over low heat in skillet. Pour in half the egg mixture. Layer half the spinach and half the shrimp on eggs. Add remaining spinach and shrimp. Pour remaining egg over top. Cook, covered, over low heat until set. Remove to serving plate. Slice to serve. Yield: 4 to 6 servings.

DOVER SOLE — England

4 sole, dressed	1 cup butter
Salt to taste	Juice of 1 lemon
Melted butter	1/2 cup chopped fresh parsley

Wash dressed fish; pat dry. Sprinkle inside and out with salt. Brush with melted butter. Grill over hot coals just until fish flakes easily, brushing with melted butter. Remove to warm platter. Melt 1 cup butter in skillet. Cook until light brown. Add lemon juice and parsley. Serve with sole. Yield: 4 servings.

SCALLOPS WITH VEGETABLES — China

2 tablespoons oil
2 onions, coarsely chopped
3 stalks celery, diagonally
    sliced
8 ounces green beans,
    diagonally sliced
2 teaspoons grated fresh
    gingerroot
1 clove of garlic, crushed

4 teaspoons cornstarch
1 cup water
2 1/2 tablespoons dry Sherry
4 teaspoons soy sauce
2 teaspoons instant chicken
    bouillon
1 pound scallops
8 ounces mushrooms, sliced
6 green onions, sliced

Heat oil in wok over high heat. Add onions, celery, beans, ginger and garlic. Stir-fry for 3 minutes. Blend cornstarch with 2 tablespoons water in small bowl. Stir in remaining water, Sherry, soy sauce and bouillon. Stir into vegetables. Cook until thickened, stirring constantly. Add scallops, mushrooms and green onions. Cook for 4 minutes or just until scallops are tender, stirring constantly.
Yield: 4 to 6 servings.

SEAFOOD AND CHICKEN STEW (PAELLA) — Spain

1 3-pound chicken, cut up
2 carrots, sliced
2 onions, cut into quarters
1 stalk celery with leaves,
    sliced
5 cups water
2 1/2 to 3 teaspoons salt
1/4 teaspoon pepper
2/3 cup long grain rice

2 cloves of garlic, crushed
1/4 cup olive oil
1/4 cup chopped pimento
1/2 teaspoon oregano
1/4 teaspoon saffron
1 10-ounce package frozen
    artichoke hearts, thawed
10 ounces peeled shrimp
1 10-ounce can clams, drained

Combine chicken with carrots, onions, celery, water, salt and pepper in heavy saucepan. Bring to a boil; reduce heat. Simmer, covered, for 1 hour or until chicken is tender. Strain stock, reserving 4 cups. Chop chicken. Sauté rice and garlic in olive oil in saucepan for 10 minutes. Add reserved stock, pimento, oregano and saffron. Simmer, covered, for 15 minutes. Add chicken, artichoke hearts, shrimp and clams. Simmer, covered, for 15 minutes. Yield: 6 servings.

BUBBLE AND SQUEAK (COLCANNON) — England

1 pound potatoes, cooked,
    mashed
1 pound cabbage, chopped,
    cooked

Salt to taste
1 medium onion, chopped
1/4 cup butter

Combine potatoes, cabbage and salt in bowl; mix well. Sauté onion in butter in heavy skillet. Add vegetable mixture. Cook for 15 to 20 minutes or until brown on bottom. Invert onto serving plate. Cut into wedges to serve.
Yield: 4 to 6 servings.

EGGPLANT CASSEROLE (MOUSSAKA) — Greece

2 onions, chopped
2 eggplant, peeled, chopped
3 tomatoes, peeled, chopped
Salt and pepper to taste
1/4 cup olive oil

5 slices bacon
1/2 cup feta cheese
1/2 cup milk
2 egg yolks
Nutmeg to taste

Sauté onions, eggplant and tomatoes with salt and pepper in olive oil over medium heat; do not brown. Layer half the eggplant mixture, bacon and remaining eggplant in deep baking dish. Combine cheese, milk and egg yolks in bowl. Beat until smooth. Add nutmeg to taste. Pour over casserole. Bake at 400° F. for 30 to 45 minutes or until eggplant is tender. Cover with foil if necessary to prevent overbrowning. Yield: 8 servings.

LENTILS WITH RICE (MJDARA) — North Africa

2 cups lentils
2 teaspoons salt
3/4 cup long grain rice

1/2 teaspoon pepper
2 onions, chopped
1/4 cup olive oil

Soak lentils in water to cover in bowl overnight. Drain. Combine with fresh water and salt in saucepan. Cook for 45 minutes. Add rice and pepper. Cook for 20 minutes or until rice is tender, adding additional water if necessary. Sauté onions in olive oil in skillet. Add to lentil mixture. May add ham, raisins, pistachios and/or chopped tomatoes if desired. Yield: 6 to 8 servings.

CREAMED MUSHROOMS (EIERSCHWAMMERL) — Austria

2 onions, chopped
1 clove of garlic, minced
1 tablespoon chopped parsley
1/2 teaspoon caraway seed
1/2 teaspoon pepper
2 tablespoons oil

1 pound mushrooms, sliced
1 tablespoon flour
3/4 cup beef bouillon
Salt to taste
1/2 cup sour cream

Sauté onions, garlic, parsley, caraway seed and pepper in oil in skillet for several minutes. Add mushrooms. Cook until liquid evaporates, stirring frequently. Sprinkle with flour. Stir in bouillon and salt. Cook until thickened, stirring gently. Stir in sour cream. Yield: 4 servings.

POTATO SOUFFLÉ
(SOUFFLÉ AUX POMMES DE TERRE) — Switzerland

4 cups hot mashed potatoes
1/2 cup Parmesan cheese
2 cups light cream

2 eggs, separated
2 teaspoons salt

Combine potatoes, cheese, cream, egg yolks and salt in bowl; mix until smooth. Cool. Beat egg whites in bowl until stiff peaks forms. Fold gently into potato mixture. Spoon into ungreased 2-quart soufflé dish. Bake at 375° F. for 50 to 60 minutes or until golden. Serve immediately. Yield: 8 servings.

SPINACH IN COCONUT MILK — Australia

1 cup shredded coconut
1 cup milk
2 pounds spinach
2 onions, chopped

1 teaspoon lemon juice
1 teaspoon salt
1/2 teaspoon pepper

Bring coconut and milk to a boil in saucepan; remove from heat. Let stand for 30 minutes. Press milk from coconut, reserving coconut for another purpose. Combine coconut milk with spinach, onions, lemon juice, salt and pepper in saucepan. Cook for 20 minutes or just until spinach is tender. Yield: 4 servings.

STIR-FRIED VEGETABLES — China

2 tablespoons oil
1 pound chopped fresh broccoli
2 onions, chopped
1 tablespoon minced gingerroot
8 ounces snow peas
8 green onions, sliced

4 stalks celery, diagonally
  sliced
8 ounces spinach, chopped
3/4 cup water
1 tablespoon instant chicken
  bouillon

Heat oil in wok over high heat. Add broccoli, onions and gingerroot. Stir-fry for 1 minute. Add remaining vegetables. Stir-fry for 1 minute. Stir in mixture of water and bouillon. Bring to a boil. Cook, covered, for 2 to 3 minutes or just until vegetables are tender-crisp. Yield: 4 to 6 servings.

TOFU AND BAMBOO SHOOTS — Japan

16 ounces tofu
1 can bamboo shoots, drained
4 eggs
1 tablespoon soy sauce

2 tablespoons Sake or white
  wine
Salt and pepper to taste

Cut tofu into cubes. Place in small greased baking dish. Spread bamboo shoots over tofu. Beat eggs with soy sauce, Sake and pepper in bowl. Pour over casserole. Bake at 400° F. for 20 minutes or until top is browned. Garnish with parsley. Yield: 2 to 4 servings.

EGG BREAD (CHALLAH) — Israel

1 package yeast
Pinch of saffron
1 cup lukewarm water
4 cups flour

2 eggs
2 teaspoons sugar
1 teaspoon salt
1 egg yolk, beaten

Combine yeast, saffron and lukewarm water in bowl. Let stand for 5 minutes. Stir in 1 cup flour. Let rise, covered, in warm place for 30 minutes. Add remaining flour, eggs, sugar and salt; mix well. Knead on floured surface until smooth and elastic. Shape into ball. Place in greased bowl; dust with flour. Let rise for 2 hours or until doubled in bulk. Knead until smooth. Divide into 3 portions. Roll into long ropes on floured surface. Braid ropes. Shape into ring on floured baking sheet. Brush with egg yolk. Let rise until doubled in bulk. Bake at 400° F. for 40 minutes or until brown. Yield: 8 servings.

FILLED SWEET ROLLS (KOLACHES) — Poland

2 packages dry yeast	4 eggs
6 tablespoons lukewarm milk	4 egg yolks
2 tablespoons sugar	4 cups sifted flour
1 teaspoon salt	Orange marmalade
1/2 cup butter, softened	Confectioners' sugar

Dissolve yeast in lukewarm milk. Stir in sugar and salt. Combine butter, 1 egg and 1 egg yolk in bowl. Beat until smooth. Add remaining eggs and egg yolks in same manner, beating well after each addition. Add yeast and flour; beat until smooth. Let rise, covered, in warm place until doubled in bulk. Shape into balls the size of large walnuts. Press indentation into each ball. Fill with marmalade. Reshape balls to enclose filling. Place 2 inches apart on greased baking sheet. Let rise for 30 minutes. Bake at 350° F. for 20 minutes. Cool. Sprinkle with confectioners' sugar. Yield: 4 dozen.

PANCAKES (PANNKAKA) — Sweden

1 1/2 cups flour	3 eggs, beaten
1/2 teaspoon salt	1/4 cup water
3 cups milk	2 tablespoons melted butter

Sift flour and salt into bowl. Add half the milk; beat until smooth. Add remaining milk, beating until smooth. Add remaining ingredients; mix well. Drop by spoonfuls onto hot greased griddle. Bake until light brown on both sides. Yield: 4 to 6 servings.

FRIED BREAD (POORI) — India

2 2/3 cups sifted flour	2 tablespoons shortening
1 2/3 cups whole wheat flour	1 1/4 cups water
2 teaspoons salt	Oil for deep frying

Combine flour, whole wheat flour and salt in bowl. Mix in shortening with fingers. Stir in water with fork until mixture forms dough. Shape into ball. Let rest for 30 minutes. Knead on floured surface for 5 minutes or until smooth. Roll 1/8 inch thick; cut into 3-inch circles. Deep-fry a few at a time in 365° oil for 30 seconds or until puffed. Turn; fry for 1 minute longer. Drain on paper towel. Yield: 4 dozen.

SCONES — Scotland

2 tablespoons butter
2 cups flour
2 teaspoons baking powder

1 teaspoon salt
2 tablespoons sugar
1 cup (scant) milk

Cut butter into mixture of dry ingredients in bowl. Stir in milk to make a sticky dough. Pat out on floured surface; cut with biscuit cutter. Bake on griddle until brown on both sides. Yield: 2 dozen.

SODA BREAD — Ireland

3 cups flour
2/3 cup sugar
1 teaspoon baking powder
1 teaspoon soda
1 teaspoon salt

1 cup raisins
2 eggs
1 1/4 cups buttermilk
2 tablespoons melted butter

Combine flour, sugar, baking powder, soda and salt in bowl. Add raisins. Beat eggs with buttermilk in small bowl. Add to dry ingredients; mix well. Stir in butter. Pour into greased 8-inch baking pan. Bake at 350° F. for 1 hour. Invert onto serving plate. Yield: 8 servings.

YORKSHIRE PUDDING — England

1 cup flour
1/2 teaspoon salt
4 eggs

1/2 cup milk
Roast beef drippings

Sift flour and salt into bowl; make well in center. Place eggs and half the milk in well. Mix with wooden spoon until smooth. Add remaining milk gradually, beating for 10 minutes. Heat roast drippings in baking pan until smoking. Add pudding batter. Bake at 400° F. until brown. Serve with roast and gravy. Yield: 6 servings.

MOORISH SPONGECAKE — Spain

3 cups flour	1¹/2 cups sugar
1 teaspoon baking powder	3 eggs
1 teaspoon salt	1 cup orange juice
¹/2 cup butter, softened	4 ounces semisweet chocolate

Sift flour, baking powder and salt together. Cream butter and sugar in mixer bowl until light. Add eggs 1 at a time, mixing well after each addition. Add dry ingredients and orange juice; mix well. Pour into 2 greased 9-inch cake pans. Bake at 375° F. for 30 minutes. Remove to serving plate. Cool for 30 minutes. Spread Frosting between layers and over top and side of cake. Melt chocolate; drizzle over cake. Yield: 8 servings.

Frosting

¹/4 cup melted butter	1 teaspoon grated orange rind
¹/4 cup orange juice	3 cups confectioners' sugar

Combine ingredients in bowl. Beat until smooth.

BIZCOCHO MORO — España

3 tazas de harina blanca	1¹/2 tazas de azúcar
1 cucharadita de polvo de hornear	3 huevos
1 cucharadita de sal	1 taza de jugo de naranja
¹/4 libre de mantequilla	4 onzas de chocolate semidulce

Cierna juntos la harina, el polvo de hornear y la sal. Bátase bien la mantequilla y el azúcar en una vasija hasta que se ponga cremosa. Añada los huevos, uno por uno, batiendo bien después de añadir cada uno. Añada los ingredientes secos y el jugo de naranja; mezcle bien. Eche la mezcla en 2 moldes engrasados de 9 pulgadas. Hornee a 375° F. por 30 minutos. Sáquelo y póngalo en una bandeja. Déjelo enfriar por 30 minutos. Ponga la mitad de la Cubierta entre los dos biscochos. Use el resto para cubrir todo el bizcocho. Derrita el chocolate semi-dulce; gotéelo sobre el bizcocho.

Cubierta

¹/4 taza de mantequilla derretida	1 cucharadita de cáscara de naranja rallada
¹/4 taza de jugo de naranja	3 tazas de azúcar pulverizado

Combine los ingredientes en una vasija. Bate bien.

BLUEBERRY CAKE — Canada

1 tablespoon shortening	4 teaspoons baking powder
3/4 cup sugar	1 teaspoon salt
1 egg	3/4 cup milk
2 cups flour	1 1/4 cups blueberries

Cream shortening and half the sugar in mixer bowl until light and fluffy. Add remaining sugar and egg; beat until smooth. Add sifted dry ingredients alternately with milk, mixing well after each addition. Fold in blueberries. Spoon into greased and floured 9-inch cake pan. Bake at 350° F. for 30 minutes or until light brown. Yield: 12 servings.

YULE LOG — England

5 eggs, separated	1 cup whipping cream
1 cup confectioners' sugar	1/4 cup confectioners' sugar
3 tablespoons baking cocoa	Chopped nuts

Grease 9 x 13-inch cake pan. Line with greased waxed paper. Beat egg yolks in mixer bowl until thick and lemon-colored. Add 1 cup confectioners' sugar and cocoa gradually, beating constantly. Beat egg whites in bowl until stiff peaks form. Fold gently into egg yolk mixture. Spread evenly in prepared pan. Bake at 350° F. for 20 minutes. Invert onto towel sprinkled with confectioners' sugar. Remove waxed paper. Roll up in towel from long side. Cool. Whip cream with 1/4 cup confectioners' sugar in mixer bowl until soft peaks form. Unroll cake; spread with whipped cream. Roll as for jelly roll. Place seam side down on serving plate. Frost with Mocha Cream Frosting. Sprinkle with nuts.
Yield: 8 servings.

Mocha Cream Frosting

1 cup unsalted butter, softened	1 tablespoon baking cocoa
1 cup confectioners' sugar	2 teaspoons coffee or Kahlua

Cream butter and confectioners' sugar in mixer bowl until light and fluffy. Add cocoa and coffee, beating until smooth.

APPLE SQUARES — Norway

2¹/₂ cups flour
1 cup sugar
1 cup margarine, softened
2 eggs

3 cups grated apples
3 tablespoons sugar
Cinnamon to taste

Combine flour, 1 cup sugar and margarine in bowl; mix well with pastry blender. Add eggs; mix until crumbly. Pat half the mixture in 9 x 13-inch baking pan. Combine apples with 3 tablespoons sugar in bowl. Spread over crumb layer. Sprinkle with cinnamon. Top with remaining crumb mixture. Bake at 375° F. for 40 to 45 minutes. Cut into squares. Yield: 12 to 14 servings.

•

BUTTER TARTS (SANDBAKELSE) — Sweden

1 cup butter, softened
1 cup sugar
1 egg

¹/₂ teaspoon almond extract
2³/₄ cups sifted flour
¹/₄ teaspoon salt

Cream butter and sugar in mixer bowl until light and fluffy. Blend in egg and almond extract. Add flour and salt gradually, mixing until smooth. Press by small amounts into sandbakelse molds. Bake at 450° F. for 5 to 7 minutes or until light brown. Invert onto rack to cool.

TOFFEE SQUARES — England

1 cup butter, softened
1 cup packed brown sugar
1 egg yolk
1 teaspoon vanilla extract
2 cups flour

¹/₄ teaspoon salt
3 or 4   7-ounce milk chocolate
   bars
¹/₂ cup chopped nuts

Cream butter, brown sugar, egg yolk and vanilla in mixer bowl until light and fluffy. Add flour and salt; mix well. Press onto 9 x 13-inch cookie sheet, leaving 1-inch edge. Bake at 350° F. for 20 to 25 minutes or until brown. Break chocolate bars into squares. Place on hot baked layer. Let stand until melted; spread evenly over top. Sprinkle with nuts. Cut into squares while warm.
Yield: 6 to 7 dozen.

BAKLAVA — Greece

1 pound walnuts, finely
   chopped
1 tablespoon sugar
1 teaspoon cinnamon
Melted butter
1 pound frozen phyllo dough,
   thawed

2 cups sugar
1 cup water
1 cinnamon stick
1/4 cup honey

Combine walnuts, 1 tablespoon sugar and cinnamon in bowl; mix well. Set aside. Brush bottom of 9 x 13-inch baking pan with butter. Layer 8 sheets of phyllo, each brushed with butter, in prepared pan. Spread half the walnut mixture over layers. Top with 2 buttered phyllo sheets and remaining walnut mixture. Layer 8 buttered phyllo sheets over top. Cut into diamond shapes. Bake at 350° F. for 30 minutes. Reduce temperature to 300° F.. Bake for 30 minutes longer. Combine 2 cups sugar, water and cinnamon stick in saucepan. Cook until mixture forms a thin syrup. Stir in honey. Remove cinnamon stick. Pour over hot pastry. Cool before serving. Yield: 24 servings.

POACHED RUBY PEARS — Canada

2 cups cranberry juice cocktail
1 cup strawberry preserves
2 4-inch cinnamon sticks

12 whole cloves
6 large firm Bartlett pears

Combine cranberry juice, strawberry preserves, cinnamon and cloves in large saucepan. Bring to a boil; reduce heat. Simmer, covered, for 15 minutes. Remove cinnamon sticks and cloves. Peel pears, leaving stems intact. Cut thin slice from bottom of each pear. Place in syrup. Simmer for 35 to 45 minutes or just until tender, turning and basting occasionally. Cool. Refrigerate pears in liquid, turning occasionally to color evenly. Remove to serving dish with slotted spoon. Use leftover syrup as marinade for fresh fruit. Yield: 6 servings.

Photograph for this recipe on Cover.

PEAR TART WITH CREAM — Spain

11 ounces frozen pastry
5 ripe pears
1 egg

3 tablespoons maple syrup
3 tablespoons sour cream
1 tablespoon sunflower seed

Thaw pastry in refrigerator overnight. Roll thin on floured surface. Place in greased tart pan, leaving edge to turn under. Prick with fork. Peel and core pears. Cut into halves, then into slices, keeping shape of pear halves. Place cut side down in prepared pan. Bake on lower shelf of oven at 400° F. for 20 minutes. Mix egg, syrup and sour cream in bowl. Pour over pears. Sprinkle with sunflower seed. Bake for 20 minutes longer. Yield: 8 servings.

TARTA DE PERAS CON CREMA — España

300 gramos de masa para
   tartas, congelada
5 peras bien maduras
1 huevo

3 cucharadas de miel de maple
3 cucharadas de crema agria
1 cucharada de semillas de
   girasol

Ponga la masa a descongelar en el refrigerador de un día para otro. Extiéndala con un rodillo enharinado hasta que esté bien delgada. Ponga en un molde engrasado, dejando un borde en las orillas que se volteará ligeramente hacia adentro. Pínchela con un tenedor. Pele las peras. Quíteles el corazón y córtelas a la mitad y luego en rebanadas, sin que pierdan su forma. Colóquelas en el molde, boca abajo. Hornéese en la parte baja del horno precalentado a 400° F. durante 20 minutos. Mezcle el huevo con la miel y la crema agria en una vasija. Viértalo entre las peras en el molde. Rocíe las semillas por encima. Hornéese otros 20 minutos.

CHEESES FROM AROUND THE WORLD

Cheese is one of the oldest foods known to man and has appeared in some form wherever he has grazed animals and used their milk. The Persian philosopher, Zoroaster, is reputed to have lived for 20 years on cheese alone in the 6th century. Cheese is frequently mentioned in the Bible. The famous Gorgonzola cheese has been made in the Po valley in Italy since 879 A.D., and the great monasteries of Europe were well known for cheese-making throughout the Middle Ages. Since that time, each country and region of the world has developed cheeses which are an integral part of their cooking and are readily identified with the cuisine of the country.

Cheese is a universal and almost perfect food. It contains many of the essential food elements which the body needs, such as proteins, fats and vitamins. The rich variety of tastes make it appealing to everyone...with the choice depending primarily on how it is to be used.

The milk from which cheese is made is separated into whey and curd. It is generally the curd which is pressed, treated, and ripened into cheese. The 2 main types of cheese are *natural* cheese and *pasteurized* process cheese products.

Natural cheeses are made by different methods; this accounts for their varying characteristics. Cheeses produced by the same method are grouped as a "family", and although textures and sharpness vary, the flavors within a family are basically similar. The nine basic cheese families are: Cheddar, Dutch, Provolone, Swiss, Bleu, Parmesan, Fresh, Surface-ripened and Whey. Natural cheeses may also be classified by texture or consistency: hard-grating, such as Parmesan; hard, such as Cheddar and Swiss; semi-soft, such as Brick and Bel Paese; soft, such as Brie and Limburger; and soft, unripened, such as cottage cheese and ricotta.

Pasteurized process cheese is made by grinding and blending one or more natural cheeses of varying strengths, then heating or pasteurizing it with an emulsifier to stop further ripening and produce cheese of uniform, consistent flavor.

The important thing to remember when cooking with cheese is that excessive heat and prolonged cooking cause it to become stringy and leathery. High heat may also cause a mixture of cheese, eggs and milk to curdle. When making a sauce, add the cheese toward the end of the cooking time, stirring over low heat just long enough to melt and blend it with the other ingredients. A cheese topping should be broiled several inches away from the heat source. Casseroles with cheese should be baked at low to medium temperatures.

One pound of shredded cheese will measure four cups for use in recipes. One pound of soft cheese such as cottage cheese or cream cheese will measure two cups.

CHEESE GUIDE

CHEESE	GOES WITH	USED FOR	FLAVOR, TEXTURE
Bel Paese (Italy)	Fresh fruit French bread	Dessert Snack	Spongy, mild, creamy yellow interior
Bleu (France)	Fresh fruit Bland crackers	Dessert Dips, salads	Marbled, blue-veined, semisoft, piquant
Brie (France)	Fresh fruit	Dessert Snack	Soft, edible crust, creamy
Brick (U.S.)	Crackers Bread	Sandwiches Snacks	Semisoft, mild, cream-colored to orange
Camembert (France)	Apples	Dessert Snack	Mild to pungent, edible crust, yellow
Cheddar (England)	Fresh fruit Crackers	Dessert Cooking, Snack	Mild to sharp, cream-colored to orange
Cottage (U.S.)	Canned or Fresh fruit	Fruit salads Cooking	Soft, moist, mild, white
Cream (U.S.)	Crackers and Jelly	Dessert, Cooking Sandwiches	Soft, smooth, mild, white
Edam (Holland)	Fresh fruit	Dessert Snack	Firm, mild, red wax coating
Feta (Greece)	Greek salad	Salad, cooking	Salty, crumbly, white
Gorgonzola (Italy)	Fresh fruit Italian bread	Dessert Snack	Semisoft, blue-veined, piquant
Gouda (Holland)	Fresh fruit Crackers	Dessert Snack	Softer then Edam, mild, nutty

CHEESE	GOES WITH	USED FOR	FLAVOR, TEXTURE
Gruyère (Switzerland)	Fresh fruit	Dessert Fondue	Nutty, bland, firm, tiny holes
Liederkranz (Germany)	Onion slices Dark Bread	Dessert Snack	Edible light orange crust, robust, soft
Limburger (Belgium)	Dark bread Bland crackers	Dessert	Soft, smooth, white, robust, aromatic
Mozzarella (Italy)	Italian foods	Cooking Pizza	Semisoft, delicate, mild, white
Muenster (Germany)	Crackers Bread	Sandwiches Snack	Semisoft, mild to mellow
Parmesan (Italy)	Italian foods	Cooking	Hard, brittle, sharp, light yellow
Port Salut (France)	Fresh fruit Crackers	Dessert Snack	Buttery, semisoft
Provolone (Italy)	Italian foods	Cooking Dessert	Salty, smoky, mild to sharp, hard
Ricotta (Italy)		Cooking Fillings	Soft, creamy, bland, white
Roquefort (France)	Bland crackers Fresh fruit	Dips, salads Dessert	Semisoft, sharp, blue-veined, crumbly
Stilton (England)	Fresh fruit Bland crackers	Dips, salads Dessert	Semisoft, sharp, blue-veined
Swiss (Switzerland)	Fresh fruit French bread	Cooking, Snack Sandwiches	Sweetish, nutty, holes, pale yellow

EQUIVALENT CHART

	When the recipe calls for:	Use:
Baking Essentials	½ cup butter	1 stick
	2 cups butter	1 pound
	4 cups all-purpose flour	1 pound
	4½ to 5 cups sifted cake flour	1 pound
	1 square chocolate	1 ounce
	1 cup semisweet chocolate pieces	1 6-ounce package
	4 cups marshmallows	1 pound
	2¼ cups packed brown sugar	1 pound
	4 cups confectioners' sugar	1 pound
	2 cups granulated sugar	1 pound
Cereal & Bread	1 cup fine dry bread crumbs	4 to 5 slices
	1 cup soft bread crumbs	2 slices
	1 cup small bread cubes	2 slices
	1 cup fine cracker crumbs	28 saltines
	1 cup fine graham cracker crumbs	15 crackers
	1 cup vanilla wafer crumbs	22 wafers
	1 cup crushed cornflakes	3 cups uncrushed
	4 cups cooked macaroni	1 8-ounce package
	3½ cups cooked rice	1 cup uncooked
Dairy	1 cup freshly grated cheese	¼ pound
	1 cup cottage cheese	1 8-ounce carton
	1 cup sour cream	1 8-ounce carton
	1 cup whipped cream	½ cup heavy cream
	⅔ cup evaporated milk	1 small can
	1⅔ cups evaporated milk	1 13-ounce can
Fruit	4 cups sliced or chopped apples	4 medium
	1 cup mashed banana	3 medium
	2 cups pitted cherries	4 cups unpitted
	3 cups shredded coconut	½ pound
	4 cups cranberries	1 pound
	1 cup pitted dates	1 8-ounce package
	1 cup candied fruit	1 8-ounce package
	3 to 4 tablespoons lemon juice plus 1 teaspoon grated rind	1 lemon
	⅓ cup orange juice plus 2 teaspoons grated rind	1 orange
	4 cups sliced peaches	8 medium
	2 cups pitted prunes	1 12-ounce package
	3 cups raisins	1 15-ounce package

When the recipe calls for:	Use:
Meats 4 cups chopped cooked chicken 3 cups chopped cooked meat 2 cups cooked ground meat	1 5-pound chicken 1 pound, cooked 1 pound, cooked
Nuts 1 cup chopped nuts	4 ounces, shelled 1 pound, unshelled
Vegetables 2 cups cooked green beans 2½ cups lima beans or red beans 4 cups shredded cabbage 1 cup grated carrots 1 4-ounce can mushrooms 1 cup chopped onion 4 cups sliced or chopped raw potatoes 2 cups canned tomatoes	½ pound fresh or 1 16-ounce can 1 cup dried, cooked 1 pound 1 large ½ pound, fresh 1 large 4 medium 1 16-ounce can

Measurement Equivalents

1 tablespoon = 3 teaspoons
2 tablespoons = 1 ounce
4 tablespoons = ¼ cup
5 tablespoons + 1 teaspoon
    = ⅓ cup
8 tablespoons = ½ cup
12 tablespoons = ¾ cup
16 tablespoons = 1 cup
1 cup = 8 ounces or ½ pint
4 cups = 1 quart
4 quarts = 1 gallon
	6½ to 8-ounce can = 1 cup
	10½ to 12-ounce can = 1¼ cups
	14 to 16-ounce can (No. 300) = 1¾ cups
	16 to 17-ounce can (No. 303) = 2 cups
	1-pound 4-ounce can or 1-pint 2-ounce can
	    (No. 2) = 2½ cups
	1-pound 13-ounce can (No. 2½) = 3½ cups
	3-pound 3-ounce can or 46-ounce can
	    = 5¾ cups
	6½-pound or 7-pound 5-ounce can (No. 10)
	    = 12 to 13 cups

Metric Equivalents

Liquid	Dry
1 teaspoon = 5 milliliters 1 tablespoon = 15 milliliters 1 fluid ounce = 30 milliliters 1 cup = 250 milliliters 1 pint = 500 milliliters	1 quart = 1 liter 1 ounce = 30 grams 1 pound = 450 grams 2.2 pounds = 1 kilogram

NOTE: The metric measures are approximate benchmarks for purposes of home food preparation.

SUBSTITUTION CHART

	Instead of:	Use:
Baking	1 teaspoon baking powder	¼ teaspoon soda plus ½ teaspoon cream of tartar
	1 tablespoon cornstarch (for thickening)	2 tablespoons flour or 1 tablespoon tapioca
	1 cup sifted all-purpose flour	1 cup plus 2 tablespoons sifted cake flour
	1 cup sifted cake flour	1 cup minus 2 tablespoons sifted all-purpose flour
	1 cup fine dry bread crumbs	¾ cup fine cracker crumbs
Dairy	1 cup buttermilk	1 cup sour milk or 1 cup yogurt
	1 cup heavy cream	¾ cup skim milk plus ⅓ cup butter
	1 cup light cream	⅞ cup skim milk plus 3 tablespoons butter
	1 cup sour cream	⅞ cup sour milk plus 3 tablespoons butter
	1 cup sour milk	1 cup milk plus 1 tablespoon vinegar or lemon juice or 1 cup buttermilk
Seasoning	1 teaspoon allspice	½ teaspoon cinnamon plus ⅛ teaspoon cloves
	1 cup catsup	1 cup tomato sauce plus ½ cup sugar plus 2 tablespoons vinegar
	1 clove of garlic	⅛ teaspoon garlic powder or ⅛ teaspoon instant minced garlic or ¾ teaspoon garlic salt or 5 drops of liquid garlic
	1 teaspoon Italian spice	¼ teaspoon each oregano, basil, thyme, rosemary plus dash of cayenne
	1 teaspoon lemon juice	½ teaspoon vinegar
	1 tablespoon mustard	1 teaspoon dry mustard
	1 medium onion	1 tablespoon dried minced onion or 1 teaspoon onion powder
Sweet	1 1-ounce square chocolate	¼ cup cocoa plus 1 teaspoon shortening
	1⅔ ounces semisweet chocolate	1 ounce unsweetened chocolate plus 4 teaspoons granulated sugar
	1 cup honey	1 to 1¼ cups sugar plus ¼ cup liquid or 1 cup corn syrup or molasses
	1 cup granulated sugar	1 cup packed brown sugar or 1 cup corn syrup, molasses or honey minus ¼ cup liquid

INDEX OF RECIPE TITLES

Translated recipe page numbers are preceeded by a T.

INDEX

160

Add To Your Cookbook Collection
or
Give As A Gift

FOR ORDERING INFORMATION

Favorite Recipes Press
a division of Great American Opportunities Inc.
P.O. Box 305142, Nashville, TN   37230
or
Call Toll-free
1-800-251-1542